RENEWAL WITHIN TRADITION

SERIES EDITOR: MATTHEW LEVERING

Matthew Levering is the James N. and Mary D. Perry, Jr. Chair of Theology at Mundelein Seminary. Levering is the author or editor of over thirty books. He serves as coeditor of the journals *Nova et Vetera* and the *International Journal of Systematic Theology*.

ABOUT THE SERIES

Catholic theology reflects upon the content of divine revelation as interpreted and handed down in the Church, but today Catholic theologians often find the scriptural and dogmatic past to be alien territory. The *Renewal within Tradition* Series undertakes to reform and reinvigorate contemporary theology from within the tradition, with St. Thomas Aquinas as a central exemplar. As part of its purpose, the Series reunites the streams of Catholic theology that, prior to the Council, separated into neo-scholastic and *nouvelle théologie* modes. The biblical, historical-critical, patristic, liturgical, and ecumenical emphases of the Ressourcement movement need the dogmatic, philosophical, scientific, and traditioned enquiries of Thomism, and vice versa. *Renewal within Tradition* challenges the regnant forms of theological liberalism that, by dissolving the cognitive content of the gospel, impede believers from knowing the love of Christ.

PUBLISHED OR FORTHCOMING

Aquinas on Beatific Charity and the Problem of Love
Christopher J. Malloy

Christ the Logos of Creation: Essays in Analogical Metaphysics
John R. Betz

On Love and Virtue: Theological Essays
Michael Sherwin, O.P.

Reading the Sermons of Aquinas: A Beginner's Guide
Randall B. Smith

The Church of Christ: According to Vatican II
Stephen A. Hipp

THE CULTURE OF
THE INCARNATION

Essays in Catholic Theology

THE CULTURE OF THE INCARNATION

Essays in Catholic Theology

TRACEY ROWLAND

EMMAUS
ACADEMIC

Steubenville, Ohio
www.emmausacademic.com

EMMAUS
ACADEMIC

Steubenville, Ohio
www.emmausacademic.com
A Division of The St. Paul Center for Biblical Theology
Editor-in-Chief: Scott Hahn
1468 Parkview Circle
Steubenville, Ohio 43952

Library of Congress Cataloging-in-Publication Data
Names: Rowland, Tracey, 1963- author.
Title: The culture of the Incarnation : essays in Catholic theology / Tracey
   Rowland.
Description: Steubenville : Emmaus Academic, 2017. | Series: Renewal within
   tradition |
Identifiers: LCCN 2017020410 (print) | LCCN 2017024714 (ebook) | ISBN
   9781945125522 (ebook) | ISBN 9781945125171 (hardcover) | ISBN
   9781945125515 (pbk.)
Subjects: LCSH: Christianity and culture. | Catholic Church--Doctrines. |
   Incarnation.
Classification: LCC BX1795.C85 (ebook) | LCC BX1795.C85 R69 2017 (print) |
   DDC 261--dc23
LC record available at https://lccn.loc.gov/2017020410

Cover image: *Jesus among the doctors*, ca. 1560, Paolo Veronese, Museo del Prado, Madrid, Spain.

Cover design and layout by Margaret Ryland

For my godson Thomas MacKinnon

TABLE OF CONTENTS

Introduction

THIS IS A COLLECTION of essays that have previously been published in separate journals over the past decade. In one way or another, they each take seriously the idea that the Incarnation was the greatest revolution in world history. When the Word became flesh, a new era of grace began, redemption from the effects of the first sin became possible, and humanity found itself in a sacramental cosmos. As St. Thomas Aquinas expressed the idea poetically, *Et antiquum documentum, Novo cedat ritui*: ancient rites have now departed; newer rites of grace prevail.

These newer rites of grace opened the gates to a Christian humanism and a whole cultural order built upon it. St. John Paul II described such a culture as a civilization of love and contrasted it with a culture of death. Pope Benedict XVI described the culture of death as a dictatorship of relativism. These two men, who were arguably two of the finest scholars ever to occupy the Chair of St. Peter, shared a quarter century of intellectual partnership. During this time, they offered the world a theological analysis of the current crisis in which Western culture finds itself. The essays in the present volume amplify this analysis.

The first essay addresses the arguments by Joseph Ratzinger/Benedict XVI against correlating the Catholic faith to the intellectual fashions and social practices of the times. The correlationist project reached the zenith of its popularity in the 1970s, though it has never completely died out and enthusiasm for the project can still be found among clergy and school teachers who came of age during the 1960s, when the project was first promoted. At the time, Ratzinger suggested that the Church is not a haberdashery shop that updates her windows with each new fashion season, and he described such projects in the field of liturgical practices as "infantile claptrap."

The second essay addresses a related topic of Ratzinger/Benedict's understanding of the world in salvation history. This was initially written in response to critics who argued that Ratzinger was hostile to the world because of his Augustinian inclinations. It is certainly the case that theologians steeped in patristic scholarship were much less likely to support correlationism than those whose early formation had been in scholasticism, and many of those with a scholastic education in their seminary did indeed buy the argument that correlationism was merely a modern analogue for what Aquinas had done with Greek thought in the thirteenth century. In this second essay, however, it is argued that these two dispositions (pro-correlationism and anti-correlationism) had little, if anything, to do with an alleged different attitude toward the world on the part of Aquinas and Augustine. The idea that theologians can be grouped into two classes, the grace sniffers and the heresy sniffers, and that Thomists are by nature grace sniffers and that Augustinians are by nature heresy sniffers, is here challenged.

The third essay is also addressed to the alleged difference in approach to the world by Thomist and Augustinian scholars, though it is not narrowly confined to the scholarship of Ratzinger as a supposed showcase of Augustinian thinking.

The fourth essay follows the trajectory set by the previous two by explaining that Ratzinger had an understanding of the theological virtue of hope different from that of secular social theorists, especially from the ideas of Ernst Bloch. Bloch did have an influence on some Catholic theologians, most notably Johann Baptist Metz, but certainly not over Ratzinger. One reason for Ratzinger's opposition to secularist analogues for the theological virtue of hope and to the whole correlationist project is that he believed that social theories are not theologically innocent. Many contemporary social theories are secularist mutations of classically Christian or Jewish ideas, and thus, to correlate the faith to them is to engage in a project of self-secularization. Such projects confuse the faithful by giving the impression that mutated concepts are consistent with Christian concepts and, so, lead to a general lowering of the intellectual horizons of the faithful, encouraging theological illiteracy as the secularist language is taken up and used in preference to specifically Catholic idioms. Each time this is done, something of the richness and complexity and even multidimensional nature of the Catholic vision is lost. This was a problem well understood by the late and great Cardinal Francis George of Chicago. In his doctoral dissertation, he concluded that "cultural forms and linguistic expressions are, in fact, not distinguished from the thoughts and message they carry as accidents are distinguished from substance in classical philosophy. A change in form inevitably entails also some change in content. A change in words changes in some fashion the way that we think."[1] The difficulty of separating concepts from their cultural traditions and transposing them into the idioms of an alternative and often rival tradition has also been a recurring theme in the philosophical works of Alasdair MacIntyre.

The fifth essay broadens the discussion by bringing in ideas from St. John Paul II and examining how the two pontiffs engaged with the concept of culture at its most general. Here, following the categories typically used in German scholarship, it is argued that culture can be examined in at least three dimensions: (i) as a civilization, or what the Germans call a *Kultur*, (ii) in the sense of *ethos* or the general character of an institution, and (iii) in the sense of what the Germans call *Bildung*, the culture or education of a person. It is further suggested that the publications of St. John Paul II offer a wealth of material on culture understood in the first and second sense, while the publications of Ratzinger/Benedict are more strongly focused on culture understood in the third sense.

The sixth essay takes the form of a lecture to World Youth Day pilgrims who were about to embark on a tour of Poland for the first time. This lecture was, therefore, written to give people born after 1989 a 101-level introduction to the Polish experience of Communism. While it is not an explicitly theological piece like the other essays, and while those with strong memories of the 1980s may well decide to skip over it, it does serve as a good introduction to the seventh essay, which is on the role of the Polish intelligentsia in the destruction of Communism. This seventh essay showcases how the Catholic faith, if followed by a significant percentage of any given population, can transform a debased, vulgar, and even brutal social order. The Polish *Solidarność* movement was all about turning a culture of death into a civilization of love.

In stark contrast to a Communist culture or a liberal culture taking the form of a dictatorship of relativism, a significant component of the culture of the Incarnation is respect for the natural moral law or human ecology. Thus, the eighth essay addresses this topic and, in particular, ways of effecting an agreement between Thomist scholars and those who approach the subject of natural law from the perspective of the nuptial mystery. Since the time this essay was published in 2008, other scholars such as Thomas Joseph White, O.P., and Edward T. Oakes, S.J., have recommended the work of Matthias Joseph Scheeben (1835–1888) as a use-

---

[1] Cardinal Francis George, *Inculturation and Ecclesial Communion: Culture and Church in the Teaching of John Paul II* (Rome: Urbaniana University Press, 1990), 47.

ful bridge between the two perspectives. Arguably the scholarship of both Servais Pinckaers, O.P. (recommended in this essay), and that of Scheeben can both form useful connections between the two groups of theologians, who are already in strong agreement that there actually *is* a natural law (postmodern philosophy notwithstanding).

The final essay was initially written for presentation at an ecumenical symposium, and it therefore addresses the ways in which a Catholic understanding of the humanism and culture of the Incarnation differs from variations to be found within Calvinist intellectual circles. It was written before the author discovered the short story "The Treading of Grapes" by the Orcadian writer George Mackay Brown (1921–1996). The story takes the form of three homilies delivered on the theme of the Wedding Feast of Cana, and this essay presents the reader with these three completely different "takes" on Christianity. The first homily, delivered in 1788 by a Calvinist Presbyterian minister, was down on every kind of human enjoyment from wine to party dresses, berating the flock for spending too much money on their wardrobes and drinking too much at weddings. This minister compares their enjoyment of ale to piglets sucking on the teats of a sow. The second homily is delivered in the twentieth century by a modern liberal Protestant minister who uses the homily to explain that Jesus did not really turn water into wine. There was no miracle: Jesus was simply a good organizer who knew that his apostles were big drinkers and that, unless he saw to it behind the scenes, supplies would be insufficient and the host of the event could have found himself embarrassed. On this account, Jesus was a responsible person and, therefore, a forward planner. Finally, one is treated to a homily by a Catholic priest delivered in 1548. Rather than being critical of the joys of life (beer, wine, and party dresses) or denying the reality of miracles, the priest tells his congregation that, at the wedding feast of the Lamb (of which Cana is merely a foreshadowing), they will all be princes. Therefore, he says, "I will call you Olaf the Fisherman and Jock the Crofter no longer but I will call you by the name the Creator will call you on the last day—Princes! Prince Olaf! Prince Jock!" Within a sacramental cosmos, not only is it possible for Christ to turn water into wine, but He can turn wine into blood and raw human beings into saints and members of a royal priesthood.

It is hard to find a better literary portrayal of the humanism of the Incarnation and the dramatic contrasts between a classically Calvinist, contemporary liberal, and a deeply Catholic cosmology. As Alison Gray wrote in *George Mackay Brown: No Separation*, "the contemplative attitude finds a 'quarry of images' in a pre-Reformation sensorium within which Mackay

Brown embraces not only a wild beauty but also vanished communities; 'the old walls of Churches and Monasteries, the defaced ruins of altars, images, and crosses do cry with a loud voice, that the Romain Catholique faith of Jesus Christ did tread this way.'" [2]

One hopes that we have not yet reached the point where one has to read short stories set in 1548 to get a sense of what the culture of the Incarnation might look like. Nonetheless, we do seem to be in the midst of an intense cosmic battle and the following essays are all variations on this theme of building a culture out of the rubble of secularist mutations so that twenty-first-century Prince Olafs and Prince Jocks (and their princesses!) might know what it means for newer rites of grace to prevail.

A final comment is that readers will find that there are two quotations that re-appear throughout the essays: *Gaudium et Spes* §22 and a statement from the International Theological Commission's document on Faith and Inculturation. The repetition of these passages was unavoidable because the essays were originally written as stand-alone pieces and the argumentation within them requires the citation of these paragraphs. It is well known that *Gaudium et Spes* §22 was cited more times by John Paul II than any other paragraph from the documents of the Second Vatican Council because it is the key to the Christocentric interpretation of the Council and to the New Evangelization favored by him and Ratzinger/Benedict.

---

[2] Alison Gray, *George Mackay Brown: No Separation* (London: Gracewing, 2016), 5.

CHAPTER 1

Beyond the Correlationist Paradigm: Joseph Ratzinger on Re-Evangelization and Mass Culture[1]

IN AN ESSAY WRITTEN IN 1962, the Munich-based Jesuit Erich Przywara observed that there is a tension or polarity between religion and culture that has run through the whole history of Christianity.[2] Beginning with Justin and Tertullian, he noted that their opposition might be categorized as the "either/or" between religion as the ultimate strength of culture and culture as religion's opponent. Similarly, he noted in the early Middle Ages the acute contrast between the monasteries of Cluny and Clairvaux and the still more acute contrast between Peter Abelard and St. Bernard. Cluny is renowned for the visual splendor of its Romanesque architecture, and Clairvaux is famous for its austerity. Abelard is remembered for his sensuality (not only because of his affair with the beautiful and brilliant Héloïse but also for the sensual beauty of his musical and poetic compositions), while it is known that it took a decision of a general chapter of St. Bernard's order to make him mitigate the austerities of his regime at Clairvaux. Przywara observed that these polarities fed into the chaos of the Reformation, in which the contrast was between the culturally resplendent Church of the Renaissance (and later the baroque period)

---

[1] Paper presented to the Fellowship of Catholic Scholars annual convention, September 26–28, 2009, Rhode Island. First published in *The Thought of Joseph Ratzinger/Pope Benedict XVI, Proceedings from the 32nd Annual Convention of the Fellowship of Catholic Scholars*, ed. K. D. Whitehead (Chicago: University of Scranton Press, 2009).

[2] Erich Przywara, *Weg zu Gott* (Einsiedeln: Johannes Verlag, 1962), 502.

and the iconoclastic "imperceptible and invisible God" of the Protestants. He concluded that nineteenth-century intellectual history was characterized by a division between the idea of the pursuit of scientific and cultural knowledge as a kind of religion in itself and the gradually ascendant ideals of the Catholic romantics of science and culture, which have their immanent ideals in religion, especially in Christendom.

Przywara had the distinction of having taught both Balthasar and Rahner and having been an early mentor for Edith Stein, but he did not attend the Second Vatican Council. He died in 1972 at the height of the post-conciliar chaos. His summary may be brought up to date by adding to it the fact that in the post-conciliar Church there has been a division between, on the one hand, those who want to baptize contemporary mass culture—a pastoral strategy promoted at the time of the Council by the *peritus* Albert Dondeyne and to a significant degree supported by Cardinal Lercaro from Bologna—and on the other, those who regard this strategy as a major cause of the dramatic decline in the numbers of those participating in the sacramental life of the Church after the Council. Indeed, in the post-conciliar era, these two positions have grown so far apart that it is no longer accurate to describe them as poles held in tension. While whole diocesan liturgical commissions spend their time trying to make the liturgical practices of the Church more closely embody elements of contemporary popular culture, there are those like Cardinal James Stafford who claim that "every world religion is trembling before the advances of American pop culture," and thus, that pop culture is actually toxic to the flourishing of faith.[3]

Ratzinger is firmly on the side of those who think like Stafford, and indeed, his opposition to the project of accommodating the cultural life of the Church to that of contemporary mass culture is possibly that element of his intellectual work for which he is most famous. Certainly no other cardinal of his generation has written so extensively on this topic. He has cautioned that where the imprint of the Catholic faith remains in a culture, one should not try to destroy it in the zeal for renewal—it should not be pushed aside as "outmoded junk."[4] In taking this stance, he has been one of the very few theologians of his generation not to follow the so-called "correlationist" pastoral strategies associated with the theology of Karl Rahner, Marie-Dominique Chenu, Edward Schillebeeckx, and David

---

[3] Cardinal James Stafford, "Knights of Columbus-States Dinner Keynote Address," Washington, DC, August 3, 2004.

[4] Joseph Ratzinger, *On the Way to Jesus Christ* (San Francisco: Ignatius Press, 2005), 45.

Tracy that sought to attach the faith to some *pierres d'attente* (toothing stones) jutting out from modern and postmodern cultural formations.

Often the argument is made that some element of these modern and postmodern formations actually had a Christian foundation and that there is thus some point within them to which the Christian faith can graft itself. However, Hans Urs von Balthasar and many of the Catholic literary figures of the first half of the twentieth century were skeptical of this kind of strategy. Balthasar represents well the stark contrast of the *Communio* theologians (principally Balthasar, Ratzinger, and de Lubac) with ideas of attaching the faith to anything that has become detached from its Christian roots:

> The Gospel and the Church are plundered like a fruit tree, but the fruits, once separated from the tree, go rotten and are no longer fruitful. The "ideas" of Christ cannot be separated from Him, and so they are of no use to the world unless they are fought for by Christians who believe in Christ, or at least by men who are inwardly, though unconsciously, open to Him and governed by Him. Radiance is only possible when the radiant centre is permanently active and alive. There can be no shining from stars long dead.[5]

Although Ratzinger has not explicitly addressed this passage from Balthasar, his comments on the theme of culture strongly resonate with it. In his own analysis, Ratzinger begins with the observation that the slate of the human mind is never blank. It bears the stamp of a community that provides patterns of thinking, feeling, and acting. In a statement that sounds evocative of Michael Polanyi's theory of "tacit" knowledge, Ratzinger defines culture as the "system of notions and thought patterns that preconditions the individual human being to judge in certain ways."[6] With Henri de Lubac, he rejects the proposition that the realm of culture can ever be theologically neutral. Culture, at its core, means an opening to the divine.[7] If the divine is not the Holy Trinity, it will be some substi-

---

[5] Hans Urs von Balthasar, *Das Ganze im Fragment: Aspekte der Geschichtestheologie*, as quoted in John Saward, "Chesterton and Balthasar: The Likeness is Greater," *Chesterton Review* 22, no. 3 (August 1996): 314.

[6] Ratzinger, *On the Way to Jesus Christ*, 44.

[7] See "Christ, Faith and the Challenge of Cultures," Address to the Presidents of the Asian Bishops Conference, March 2–5, 1993; accessed March 7, 2017, http://www.ewtn.com/library/CURIA/RATZHONG.HTM.

tute for it. The Catholic faith is not some intellectual system that can be tied on to and expressed in any cultural form. For Ratzinger, "the Church is its own cultural subject for the faithful."[8] He expressly rejects the idea that national or historical cultures might allocate their own body to the faith. According to such a vision, the faith would always have to live from borrowed cultures that remain, in the end, somehow external and capable of being cast off. The culture of such a faith and its practices would be debased, becoming "a mere exchangeable shell," and the faith itself would be reduced to the standing of "a disincarnated spirit ultimately void of reality."[9] Such modes of thinking are typical of the eighteenth century, reducing culture to mere form and religion to either pure emotion or pure thought.[10] Ratzinger prefers the expression "interculturality" (the meeting of two different cultures and a constructive search for the truth embodied in both) to "inculturation" (which may imply the notion of attaching the faith to a new exchangeable shell).

Ratzinger believes that the uniqueness of Christian culture is rooted in the Incarnation and that all of its specific characteristics disintegrate when this belief is eclipsed.[11] The Incarnation means that the invisible God enters into the visible world so that those who are bound to matter can know him. In §22 of Vatican II's *Gaudium et Spes*, the significance of the Incarnation is expressed in the following manner: "The Truth is that only in the mystery of the incarnate Word does the mystery of man take on light. For Adam, the first man, was a figure of Him who was to come, namely Christ the Lord. Christ, the final Adam, by the revelation of the mystery of the Father, and His Love, fully reveals man to man himself and makes his supreme calling clear."[12]

Ratzinger further observes that the Incarnation is rightly understood only when it is seen within the broader context of creation, history, and the new world. Only then does it become clear that the senses belong to faith and that the new seeing does not abolish them, but leads them to their original purpose.[13] The International Theological Commission, under Ratzinger's leadership, expressed the position in the following paragraph:

---

[8] Ibid.

[9] Ibid.

[10] Ibid.

[11] Joseph Ratzinger, *Co-Workers of the Truth* (San Francisco: Ignatius Press, 1992), 18–19.

[12] English translation from the Vatican website.

[13] Aidan Nichols, *Say It Is Pentecost* (Edinburgh: T & T Clark, 2001), 3.

In the last times inaugurated at Pentecost, the risen Christ, Alpha and Omega, enters into the history of peoples: from that moment, the sense of history and thus of culture is unsealed and the Holy Spirit reveals it by actualizing and communicating it to all. The Church is the sacrament of this revelation and its communication. It re-centres every culture into which Christ is received, placing it in the axis of the world which is coming, and restores the union broken by the Prince of this world. Culture is thus eschatologically situated; it tends towards its completion in Christ, but it cannot be saved except by associating itself with the repudiation of evil.[14]

The theme of the relationship between religion and culture was strong in the works of the intellectual heroes of Ratzinger's youth, particularly in the personalism of Martin Buber and the theology of Romano Guardini. Buber argued that all great civilizations are based on an "original relational incident" (for example, the revelation on Mt. Sinai as recorded in the Exodus narrative or the Incarnation and Paschal Mysteries as recorded in the Gospels) and that this original relational incident creates a special conception of the cosmos that is then handed down to succeeding generations. If, however, a culture ceases to be centered in the living and continually renewed relational event, if it suffers a loss of piety, then it hardens into a world of disenchanted commodities. It becomes a kind of anticulture. Balthasar later wrote of Buber:

Those of us who know him at all realize that he is not simply another writer of Jewish race who has been admitted into the German pantheon, but the man, and, what is more, the only one, who remained in the forefront of German literature throughout the last half century, representing the Jewish race in the face of a blind hatred of everything Jewish. Unlike so many others he did not pursue a strategy of assimilation but he endeavoured to "recapture the essential spirit of Judaism."[15]

---

[14] International Theological Commission, *Faith and Inculturation* (1988), II ("Inculturation in the History of Salvation"), §28, accessed March 7, 2017, http://www.vatican.va/roman_curia/congregations/cfaith/cti_documents/rc_cti_1988_fede-inculturazione_en.html.

[15] Hans Urs von Balthasar, *Martin Buber and Christianity: A Dialogue between Israel and the Church* (London: Harvill Press, 1960), 9.

A parallel judgment can be made of Ratzinger. For him, the original relational incidents at Sinai, Nazareth, Bethlehem, and Golgotha have generated a particular conception of the cosmos and it is the duty of the Church to hand it down, undiluted, to successive generations. These incidents determine the "essential spirit of Christianity" and are constitutive of culture, rather than being something to be grafted onto an alien culture or one that has forgotten or rejected them. Thus, Ratzinger has written:

> When people rightly call for a new dialogue between the Church and culture today, they must not forget in the process that this dialogue must necessarily be bilateral. It cannot consist in the Church finally subjecting herself to modern culture, which has been caught up to a large extent in a process of self-doubt since it lost its religious base. Just as the Church must expose herself to the problems of our age in a radically new way, so too must culture be questioned anew about its groundlessness and its ground, and in the process be opened to a painful cure, that is, to a new reconciliation with religion since it can get its lifeblood only from there.[16]

Significantly, Ratzinger has not limited his criticisms of contemporary Western culture to those elements within it that are explicitly associated with what John Paul II called the culture of death. Along with many postmoderns, Ratzinger sees the contemporary phenomenon of "mass culture" as a hindrance to spiritual development, or as the postmoderns might say, a barrier to explorations in self-transcendence. The human person is becoming a commodity. As Václav Havel explained the phenomenon, "on the one hand everything is getting better all the time—a new generation of mobile phones is being released every week. But in order to make use of it you need to follow new instructions. So you end up reading instruction manuals instead of books and in your free time you watch TV where handsome tanned guys scream from advertisements about how happy they are to have new swimming trunks by fashion house X."[17]

In his collection of essays on *The End of the Modern World*, Romano Guardini drew a connection between the character of "mass man" and the problems of evangelization in the contemporary world. He described

---

[16] Joseph Ratzinger, *A New Song for the Lord: Faith in Christ and Liturgy Today* (New York: Crossroad, 1996), 96.

[17] Václav Havel, "After the Velvet: An Existential Revolution?" *Gazeta Wyborcza* 20, no. 11 (2008).

"mass man" as having no desire for independence or originality in either the management or the conduct of his life—neither liberty of external action nor freedom of internal judgment seem for him to have unique value.[18] He identified the problem as a causal relationship between the lack of a "fruitful and lofty culture" that provides the sub-soil for a healthy nature and a spiritual life that is "numb and narrow" and develops along "mawkish, perverted and unlawful lines."[19]

Although a concern about mass culture has been variously criticized as bourgeois and elitist, especially from those influenced by liberation theology, in an interview given in 1985, Ratzinger remarked that a theologian who "does not love art, poetry, music and nature can be dangerous since blindness and deafness toward the beautiful are not incidental: they are necessarily reflected in his theology." He has also said that "the only really effective apologia for Christianity comes down to two arguments, namely, the *saints* the Church has produced and the *art* which has grown in her womb."[20] Even more specifically, he has written that the greatness of Western music (from Gregorian chant to polyphony, to the Baroque age, to Bruckner, and beyond) is, for him, "the most immediate and the most evident verification that history has to offer of the Christian image of mankind and of the Christian dogma of redemption."[21]

This is not a novel position in the Catholic tradition but follows a long line of authorities, including St. Augustine, St. Bonaventure, Hugh of St. Victor, John Henry Newman, and on to Balthasar, who have regarded the aesthetic moment as essentially *theophanic*. Behind these stand the influence of Plato, for whom the beautiful and the good, ultimately the beautiful and God, coincide. In this context, Ratzinger has been influenced by what he terms "the magnificent interpretation of Platonic *eros* in Josef Pieper's *Begeisterung und göttlicher Wahnsinn: Über den platonischen Dialog Phaidros*."[22] Ratzinger summarizes Plato on this point thus: "through the appearance of the beautiful we are wounded in our innermost being, and that wound grips us and takes us beyond ourselves; it stirs longing into flight and moves us toward the truly Beautiful, to the Good in itself."[23]

---

[18] Romano Guardini, *The End of the Modern World* (London: Sheed & Ward, 1957), 78.

[19] Ibid., 88–89.

[20] Joseph Ratzinger, *The Ratzinger Report* (San Francisco: Ignatius Press, 1985), 129.

[21] *L'Osservatore Romano* 16, no. 6 (1986): 10ff.

[22] Josef Pieper, *Werke*, vol. 1, *Darstellung und Interpretationem: Platon*, ed. B. Wald (Hamburg: Meiner, 2002).

[23] Joseph Ratzinger, *The Spirit of the Liturgy* (San Francisco: Ignatius Press, 2000), 126–27.

Ratzinger also quotes the fourteenth-century Byzantine theologian Nicholas Cabasilas: "When men have a longing so great that it surpasses human nature and eagerly desire and are able to accomplish things beyond human thought, it is the Bridegroom himself who has wounded them. Into their eyes he himself has sent a ray of his beauty. The rise of the wound is evidence of the arrow, and the longing points to the one who has shot the arrow."[24] Ratzinger further notes that Cabasilas distinguished between two different kinds of knowledge: knowing through instruction, which remains secondhand and does not put the knower in contact with reality itself, and knowing through personal experience, through contact with the things themselves.[25] Ratzinger acknowledges the importance of the first form of knowledge, which he associated with the discipline of theology, but adds that we must not despise the impact produced by the heart's encounter with beauty or reject it as a true form of knowledge. To do so, he suggests, would be to "dry up both faith and theology."[26]

In *The Spirit of the Liturgy*, Ratzinger applies this Platonic theory to a broad-brush history of Western art. He argues that, in the art of icons, as well as in the great Western paintings of the Romanesque and Gothic periods, the experience described by Cabasilas has gone from being an interior event to being an external form and, thus, has become communicable.[27] However, he observes that "this kind of Platonism, transformed as it is by the Incarnation, largely disappears from the West after the thirteenth century, so that now the art of painting strives first and foremost to depict events that have taken place, rather than being essentially epiphanic."[28] With the Renaissance, "we see the development of the aesthetic in the modern sense, the vision of a beauty that no longer points beyond itself but is content in the end with itself, the beauty of the appearing thing."[29] At the same time, a nostalgia for the pre-Christian gods emerges, for a world without the pain of the Cross and the fear of sin, which Ratzinger suggests may have become too overpowering in the images of the late Middle Ages.[30] Today, he concludes, Christian art stands between two fires: "It must oppose the cult of the ugly, which says that everything else, anything beautiful, is a deception and that only the depiction of what is cruel, base,

---

[24] Ratzinger, *On the Way to Jesus Christ*, 35.

[25] Ibid., 36.

[26] Ibid.

[27] Ibid., 37.

[28] Joseph Ratzinger, "Art, Image and Artists," *Adoremus Bulletin* 8, no. 1 (March 2002): 1.

[29] Ratzinger, *The Spirit of the Liturgy*, 129.

[30] Ibid.

and vulgar is the truth and true enlightenment. And it must withstand the deceptive beauty that diminishes man instead of making him great and that, for that very reason, is false."[31]

While the art of painting in the post-Renaissance era has to some degree lost this erotic quality (understood in a Platonic sense), Ratzinger believes that music has suffered an even greater diminution of its epiphanic potential. A common theme in his many reflections on what is wrong with contemporary music is that it has become a product that can be industrially manufactured. He is not opposed to popular music per se—there is nothing inherently wrong in something being popular—but he notes that the audience to whom much contemporary pop music refers is mass society. In contrast, folk music, which he thinks is far preferable, "is the musical expression of a clearly defined community held together by its language, history, and way of life, which assimilates and shapes its experiences."[32] He notes that "such a community's way of structuring music may be naïve, but it does at least have the merit of springing from original contact with the fundamental experiences of human existence and is therefore an expression of truth."[33] Its naiveté, Ratzinger concludes, belongs to that kind of simplicity from which great things can come. Mass society, on the contrary, is something completely different from that community bound together for life that produced folk music in the old and original sense. The masses as such do not know experiences firsthand; they only know reproduced and standardized experiences. Mass culture is thus geared to quantity, production, and success. It is a culture of the measurable and the marketable.

When these criticisms are applied to the liturgical context, Ratzinger rejects the idea, popular with evangelical Protestants and many contemporary Catholic liturgists, that form and substance can be easily separated and, thus, that the only problem with rock music from a Christian point of view is the explicitly sexual and sometimes crude lyrics. He finds the music itself objectionable and claims that it has no place in the liturgy. In various publications, he recommends Calvin M. Johansson's *Music and Ministry*.[34] In this work Johansson identifies a tendency of liturgists to oscillate between the poles of aestheticism and pragmatism. He defines aestheticism

---

[31] Ratzinger, *On the Way to Jesus Christ*, 40.

[32] Ratzinger, *A New Song for the Lord*, 107.

[33] Ibid.

[34] C. M. Johansson, *Music and Ministry: A Biblical Counterpoint* (Peabody, MA: Hendrickson, 1998).

as a preoccupation with beauty for its own sake that runs into the danger of idolatry, while pragmatism creates a false dichotomy between medium and message, between music and gospel, in which each may go its own way without regard for the other.[35] The pragmatist "uses music uncritically as a message lubricator, sweetener or psychological conditioner" and "emasculates the gospel by using commercialized music to sell it."[36] Such a medium, he argues, "kills the message."[37]

Similarly Ratzinger uses the expression "utility music" to describe popular music that is used in Church services as a carrot to entice worshippers and the expression "pastoral pragmatism" for the intellectual defense of this practice. He also uses the expression "sacro-pop," which he takes from H. J. Burbach's articles in the *Internationale katholische Zeitschrift*.[38] In Ratzinger's *The Feast of Faith* and *A New Song for the Lord*, one can find passionate criticisms of "sacro-pop," "parish tea-party liturgies," "pastoral pragmatism," "primitive emotionalism," and "utility music." He acknowledges that Karl Rahner and many other Catholic intellectuals of the conciliar generation were of the view that there is nothing wrong with the use of utility music, but he disagrees. He quotes Theodor Adorno's judgment that "the fundamental characteristic of popular music is standardization" and describes this as "incompatible with the culture of the Gospels, which seek[s] to take us out of the dictatorship of money, of making, of mediocrity, and brings us to the discipline of truth, which is precisely what pop music eschews."[39] He rhetorically asks whether it is a pastoral success when Catholics are capable of following the trend of mass culture and, thus, share the blame for its making people immature or irresponsible.[40]

Even more dramatically, Ratzinger has declared that the trivialization of the faith by following the trends of mass culture "is not a new inculturation, but the denial of its culture and prostitution with the non culture."[41] He observes that disputes about music are at least as old as the conflict between Dionysian and Apollonian music in classical Greece, and that, while Apollo is not Christ, Plato's concern about the music of the Dionysian cults remains relevant today, since contemporary musical forms have become a

---

[35] Ibid., 55.
[36] Ibid., 5.
[37] Ibid.
[38] H. J. Burbach, "Sacro-pop," *Internationale katholische Zeitschrift* 3 (1974):148–57.
[39] Ratzinger, *A New Song for the Lord*, 108.
[40] Ibid., 109.
[41] Ibid.

"decisive vehicle of a counter religion."[42] Rock concerts are "anti-liturgies where people are yanked out of themselves and where they can forget the dullness and commonness of everyday life."[43] They are enterprises to make money out of the human need for an experience of self-transcendence:

> People are, so to speak, released from themselves by the experience
> of being part of a crowd and by the emotional shock of rhythm,
> noise and special lighting effects. However, in the ecstasy of hav-
> ing all their defenses torn down, the participants sink, as it were,
> beneath the elemental force of the universe. The music of the
> Holy Spirit's sober inebriation seems to have little chance when
> the self has become a prison, the mind is a shackle, and breaking
> out from both appears as a true promise of redemption that can be
> tasted at least for a few moments.[44]

In a dissertation on dogmatic theology and the ecclesial practice of music, J. Andrew Edwards concludes that Ratzinger's concern with the philosophical anthropology reflected in Dionysian music leads into his concern that music's portrayal of subjectivity may point toward a soteriology that is alien to the Christian position.[45] In other words, rock music is seeking freedom in ways that are contrary to Christian notions of freedom and responsibility. Edwards notes that Ratzinger's antagonism toward rock music is "not therefore an aesthetic decision based on his own subjective taste, but is rooted in his detection of theological doctrines lying beneath the surface of these musical practices which are diametrically opposed to the Christian faith."[46] In particular, Edwards concludes that Ratzinger's use of the Apollonian–Dionysian paradigm flows from his concern that rock music's engagement with the body may contradict the incarnational emphasis on the rational Word redeeming the sensual.[47]

It is difficult to find other such sustained critiques of the rock music industry in Catholic theological circles, though the non-Catholic English philosopher Roger Scruton has reached conclusions similar to Ratzinger's

---

[42] Ibid., 123–24.

[43] Ibid., 32.

[44] Joseph Ratzinger, "Liturgy and Sacred Music," *Communio: International Catholic Review* 13 (1986): 377–91, at 387.

[45] J. A. Edwards, "*Fides ex Auditu*: Dogmatic Theology and the Ecclesial Practice of Music" (M. Phil diss., University of St. Andrews, 2008), 95.

[46] Ibid.

[47] Ibid., 97.

in his cultural studies and the Anglican theologian Catherine Pickstock has written theological analyses of recent music history that resonate with some of Ratzinger's concerns.[48] In a lecture delivered in Cambridge on the morality of pop, Scruton argued that much contemporary pop music arrests its listeners in a state of adolescent psychological development. In the essay "Youth Culture's Lament," he describes the pop star as someone who excites his fans to every kind of artificial ecstasy, knowing that nothing will change for the fan, that the void will always remain unfulfilled. In words that could have been written by Ratzinger, he concludes:

> This music is not designed for listening. It is the accompanying soundtrack to a drama, in which the singer, strange as it may seem, becomes something like the sacred presence of a cult, the incarnation of a force beyond music, which visits the world in human form, recruiting followers the way religious leaders recruit their sects. The pop star's appearance on stage is not like that of an orchestra or an actor: it is a "real presence," an incarnation of an otherworldly being, greeted by a release of collective emotion comparable to the Dionysiac orgies depicted by Euripides.[49]

Scruton also argues that to possess a culture is not only to possess a body of knowledge or expertise, to have accumulated facts, references, and theories. It is to possess a sensibility, a response, and a way of seeing things that is in some way redemptive.[50] Thus, culture is not merely a matter of academic knowledge, but of a mode of participation that changes not only thoughts and beliefs but perceptions and emotions. To put this in the language of theological anthropology, the cultural practices in which we participate do have an effect on our capacity for self-transcendence. This is a very MacIntyrean idea, and there are arguably many points of convergence between MacIntyre and Ratzinger on the subject of the role of practices in the formation of the self and the manner in which the faith or Tradition is handed on from one generation to another. Most significant here is the reference to an interpreting community.

---

[48] Roger Scruton, *The Aesthetics of Music* (Oxford: Oxford University Press, 1999); Catherine Pickstock, "God and Meaning in Music: Messiaen, Deleuze and the Musico-Theological Critique of Modernism and Postmodernism," *Sacred Music* 134, no. 4 (2007): 40–62.

[49] Roger Scruton, "Youth Culture's Lament," *City Journal*, Autumn 1998, 15.

[50] Roger Scruton, *The Philosopher on Dover Beach: Essays* (South Bend, IN: St. Augustine's Press, 1997), 106.

Contemporary hermeneutical scholarship has emphasized the principle that thinking always involves thinking in the context of some particular and specific public, which will normally have its own institutional structure.[51] Alasdair MacIntyre has referred to the institutional structure of Plato's Academy and Aquinas's Dominican Order and to the differences between English culture and Highland Gaelic culture and the "public" of each of these. Similarly, Hans Georg Gadamer argued in *Truth and Method* that human beings always operate from within the horizons of particular languages and traditions, and thus, "meaning is not an objective property of the text that the interpreter discovers so much as an event in the present, a 'fusion of horizons.'"[52] When applied to the Scriptures, this means that the Scriptures must be interpreted from within the horizon of faith itself, and from Ratzinger's point of view, the institution of the Church and her interpretations of the passages forms part of that horizon. Ratzinger has written that "the exegete must realize that he does not occupy a neutral position above or outside Church history and he must acknowledge that the faith is the hermeneutic, the locus of understanding, which does not dogmatically force itself upon the Bible, but is the only way of letting it be itself."[53] This principle is something that he has taken from Guardini's *Das Christbild*; Ratzinger has stated that "the reflections on method that Guardini develops on pages 7–15 are among the most important things that have ever been said on the problem of methodology in scriptural interpretation."[54] Ratzinger has summarized Guardini's horizons in the following terms:

> For Guardini the first step is always attentive listening to the message of the scriptural text. In this way the real contribution of exegesis to an understanding of Jesus is fully acknowledged. But in this attentiveness to the text, the listener, according to Guardini's understanding, does not make himself to be the Master of the Word. Rather, the listener makes himself the believing disci-

---

[51] See, for example, Alasdair MacIntyre, "Some Enlightenment Projects Reconsidered," in *Questioning Ethics: Contemporary Debates in Philosophy*, ed. R. Kearney and M. Dooley (London: Routledge, 1998), 245–58, at 250.

[52] Kevin J. Vanhoozer, "Scripture and Tradition," in *The Cambridge Companion to Postmodern Theology* (Cambridge: Cambridge University Press, 2003), 152–53.

[53] Joseph Ratzinger, "Biblical Interpretation in Crisis," in *Opening Up the Scriptures: Joseph Ratzinger and the Foundations of Biblical Interpretation*, ed. J. Granados et al. (Grand Rapids, MI: Eerdmans, 2008), 29.

[54] Joseph Ratzinger, "Guardini on Christ in our Century," *Crisis Magazine*, June 1996, 14.

ple who allows himself to be led and enlightened by the Word. It is precisely by repudiating a closed merely human logic that the greatness and uniqueness of his Person becomes apparent to us. It is precisely in this way that the prison of our prejudice is broken open; it is in this way that our eyes are slowly opened, and that we come to recognize what is truly human, since we have been touched by the very humanity of God himself.[55]

A significant consequence of these principles is that those who are interested in what John Paul II called the "new evangelization" must be wary of thinking of evangelization as a project to be realized in the same sense that Communist thought promotes a culture of atheism by reference to slogans and "five-year plans." In particular, the faith cannot be packed into fashionable sound bites and concepts borrowed from the mass culture and then marketed to people without a sacramental life. Ratzinger has been critical of Karl Rahner's theology for fostering these kinds of pastoral projects that have proliferated in the wealthier dioceses of the world since the Council.[56] Of such approaches to evangelization, Ratzinger wrote:

> In the attempt to give Christianity a new interpretation through the use of short formulas, the wrong end of the problem has been seized: the slogan, a borrowing from the *instrumentarium* of consumer economics, explains nothing where there is a question of transmitting knowledge of the faith. . . . No one has ever used the formulas of the faith in the Old and New Testaments for purposes of "advertising." To do so would have been impossible, in any case, since they are concentrated summaries of the faith and can, therefore, be understood only from within the faith. In general, we can assume that the beginning of a conversion to Christianity was not likely to consist in a request for a program but rather in a favorable attitude—that was frequently directly fostered by personal relationships with Christians.[57]

---

[55] Ibid.

[56] One recent example from an Australian archdiocese was called "Contemplate and Launch Out," with posters bearing these words appearing all over archdiocesan buildings. Some had the "a" scratched out of launch, making it "lunch out," and there were a few other less polite variations found for "contemplate."

[57] Joseph Ratzinger, *Principles of Catholic Theology* (San Francisco: Ignatius Press, 1987), 128.

This is another way of saying that, for Ratzinger, evangelization, like scriptural analysis, needs to take place within a really existing Catholic community with really existing sacramental practices. The truth of the faith is revealed in the splendor of the culture that it creates, and in particular in the beauty of the saints that it produces. It cannot be marketed in any conventional sense. To arrive at this point, one needs to challenge the presumption that mass culture is theologically neutral, and one also needs to resist the temptation to think that, with better marketing, the message might be more attractive. In the following statements Ratzinger is critical of the contemporary trend of running the Church and her pastoral works as if it were a modern corporation:

> Saints, in fact reformed the Church in depth, not by working up plans for new structures, but by reforming themselves. What the Church needs in order to respond to the needs of man in every age is holiness, not management.[58]

> The saints were all people of imagination, not functionaries of apparatuses.[59]

> I have said very often that I think we have too much bureaucracy. Therefore, it will be necessary in any case to simplify things. Everything should not take place by way of committees; there must even also be the personal encounter.[60]

> Paul was effective, not because of brilliant rhetoric and sophisticated strategies, but rather because he exerted himself and left himself vulnerable in the service of the Gospel.[61]

Thus, common to Ratzinger, Guardini, and Balthasar is the idea that "in the crisis of culture we are experiencing, it is only from islands of spiritual concentration that a new cultural purification and unification can break out."[62] This is one of the two reasons given for Ratzinger's choice of

---

[58] Ratzinger, *The Ratzinger Report*, 53.

[59] Ibid., 67.

[60] Joseph Ratzinger, *Salt of the Earth: The Church at the End of the Millennium—An Interview with Peter Seewald* (San Francisco: Ignatius, 1997), 266.

[61] Joseph Ratzinger, *Images of Hope: Meditations on Major Feasts* (San Francisco: Ignatius Press, 2006), 26.

[62] Ratzinger, *A New Song for the Lord*, 126.

the papal name Benedict. In part, he wanted to honor Benedict XV, who tried so hard to bring an end to the First World War before it claimed the lives of millions of Christians on both sides of the trenches, but his second reason was his belief that Western culture needs a new Benedictine moment. Just as it was the formation of Benedictine monasteries across the map of Europe that created the first high Christian culture, today, he believes, the banality of mass culture and the anti-memory orientation of modernity will be transcended only by islands of spiritual excellence. Balthasar poignantly expressed the same idea when he wrote, "Those who withdrew to the heights to fast and pray in silence are ... the pillars bearing the spiritual weight of what happens in history. They share in the uniqueness of Christ, in the freedom of that nobility which is conferred from above; that serene, untamed freedom which cannot be caged or put to use. Theirs is the first of all aristocracies, source and justification for all the others, and the last yet remaining to us in a most unaristocratic world."[63]

In the final analysis, it would seem that Ratzinger is personally more inclined to the high cultural richness of Cluny than to the austerity of Clairvaux, but he would no doubt recognize the cultures symbolized by these two monasteries, as Przywara did, as poles held in a creative tension. The commodification of art, music, and even human beings that is typical of contemporary mass culture is not, however, something to which he believes the Church should lend her support. It has no toothing stones that might support the weight of the Catholic faith. The faith is not a product, and it cannot be packaged and marketed. It can only be lived and loved and shared with others as a gift.

---

[63] Hans Urs von Balthasar, *A Theology of History* (San Francisco: Ignatius Press, 1994), 125.

CHAPTER 2

The World in the Theology of Joseph Ratzinger/Pope Benedict XVI[1]

A TABLOID CARICATURE of Joseph Ratzinger/Benedict XVI is that he has imbibed too much of the thought of St. Augustine, leaving him with a neo-Manichean stance of hostility toward the world. A related caricature draws Catholics into two camps, what could be termed the "grace sniffers" (seeking out correlations thought to be indicative of grace already operative in the world before the sacraments) and the "heresy sniffers" (ferreting out claims of such correlations and grace that might indicate heresy), with the former Prefect of the Congregation for the Doctrine of the Faith presented as the captain of the latter. A third caricature is that Joseph Ratzinger was so shocked by the student demonstrations at the University of Tübingen in 1968 that he has developed a pathological fear of "the world" ever since. These various personality profiles are not only off-balance but also fail to engage with Ratzinger/Benedict's actual academic work on the issue of the relationship between the Church and the world and the Church and the cultures of modernity and postmodernity. Contrary to these distorted character sketches, a number of scholars who are not generally in agreement with Ratzinger's theological framework nonetheless do acknowledge that Ratzinger's theology does exhibit a quality of consistency over the decades and that theological baselines do not move in response to world events.

Joseph A. Komonchak, for example, has written that "from Ratzinger's *Introduction to Christianity* (1968) down to the homily he delivered on his

---

[1]   First published in *The Journal of Moral Theology* 2, no. 2 (June 2013): 109–33, submitted to the editor in the final week of the papacy of Benedict XVI.

installation as Pope Benedict XVI, a distinctive and consistent approach has been visible."[2] Similarly, at the time of Ratzinger's election to the papacy, when all kinds of wild claims were being made, Francis Schüssler Fiorenza (who had been a student of Ratzinger) wrote that "the negative slogans are wrong, the personal descriptions are true, and the biographical explanations are, in general, misleading. They overlook that Ratzinger has from early days had a consistent theological vision."[3] Finally, Lieven Boeve and Gerard Mannion have concluded that "Ratzinger's theological insights have not fundamentally changed, but have rather demonstrated a firm internal consistency throughout more than fifty years."[4]

The purpose of this article is therefore to situate the work of Ratzinger/Benedict in the context of early-twentieth-century German Catholic Augustinian studies, which was far removed from earlier German Protestant appropriations of the thought of St. Augustine, and to further present a summary of his theological understanding of the concept "the world" in the context of rival interpretations of *Gaudium et Spes*, the Second Vatican Council's Pastoral Constitution on the Church in Modern World.

The young Joseph Ratzinger's appropriation of the thought of St. Augustine was mediated through the scholarship of Fritz Hofmann, Erich Przywara, Romano Guardini, Gottlieb Söhngen, and Henri de Lubac.[5] Hofmann was Professor of Theology at the University of Würzburg, and in 1933, he published a seminal work on the ecclesiology of St. Augustine that the young Ratzinger read in preparation for his own doctoral disserta-

---

[2] Joseph A. Komonchak, "The Church in Crisis: Pope Benedict's Theological Vision," *Commonweal*, June 3, 2005, 11–14.

[3] Francis Schüssler Fiorenza, "From Theologian to Pope: A Personal View Back, Past and Public Portrayals," *Harvard Divinity Bulletin* 33 (2005).

[4] Lieven Boeve and Gerard Mannion, *The Ratzinger Reader* (London: Continuum, 2010), 12. Nonetheless, Boeve and Mannion do observe that Ratzinger's tone of writing became more polemical after 1968.

[5] Works that would have affected Ratzinger were, for example: Erich Przywara, "St. Augustine in the Modern World," in *A Monument to Saint Augustine: Essays on Some Aspects of His Thought Written in Commemoration of His 15th Centenary*, ed. Martin D'Arcy (London: Sheed & Ward, 1945; originally1930), 251–86; Fritz Hofmann, *Der Kirchenbegriff des hl. Augustinus in seinen Grundlagen und in seiner Entwicklung* (Munich: Max Hueber, 1933); Gottlieb Söhngen, "Wissenschaft und Weisheit im augustinischen Gedankengefüge," in *Die Einheit in der Theologie* (Munich: K. Zink, 1952); Romano Guardini, *Die Bekehrung des Aurelius Augustinus: Der innere Vorgang in seinen Bekenntnissen* (Munich: Grünewald, 1945), in English as *The Conversion of St. Augustine* (Chicago: Regnery, 1966); Henri de Lubac, *Catholicism and the Common Destiny of Man* (San Francisco: Ignatius Press, 1988).

tion, "The People of God and the House of God in the works of St. Augustine." In that work, Hofmann paid particular attention to the role of grace and the role of the Holy Spirit in the life of the Church. His treatment of Augustinian ecclesiology was followed in 1940 by another Augustinian reflection, this time on the "God is Love" theme, which was later to become the title of Benedict's first encyclical.[6]

In the interbellum period, Przywara (1889–1972) was also publishing material on Augustine and was one of the most influential German-speaking Jesuits of the twentieth century. He was a teacher of both Karl Rahner and Hans Urs von Balthasar and a spiritual director of the Carmelite martyr and Jewish convert philosopher Edith Stein. Przywara was also, for a time, the editor of the influential journal *Stimmen der Zeit* and one of those responsible for having the works of John Henry Newman translated into German. In all, he wrote some sixty books and six hundred articles. These included: *Crucis mysterium: Das christliche Heute* (1939), a work that was later praised by Ratzinger, and *Humanitas: der Mensch, Gestern und Morgen* (1952), which is a major reflection on anthropology. For Przywara, the most perfect reincarnation of Augustinianism in the modern world was to be found in the writing of John Henry Newman. Przywara concluded that Newman "settles accounts with the Reformation more thoroughly than Hegel and Kierkegaard" and "prophetically anticipated the conviction, born of the fiascos of Lausanne, Stockholm, and Malines, that the Reformation cannot be overcome by 'negotiations' of any kind, but only by a thoroughgoing reversal of 'first principles.'"[7] There was, in short, nothing remotely Protestant about Przywara's appropriation of Augustine.

The same can also be said of the Augustinian appropriations of Romano Guardini (1885–1968), who was Professor at the University of Munich from 1948 to 1962 and, thus, an important figure during the years when Ratzinger was a seminarian. Karl Rahner described Guardini as a Christian humanist who led Germany's Catholics out of an intellectual and cultural ghetto and into the contemporary world.[8] Balthasar said of Guardini that he believed that "it is not Christ who is in the world, but the world is in Christ," and further, that the "immensity of this reversal" was "the

---

[6] Fritz Hofmann, *Gott ist die Liebe: die Predigten des. Hl. Augustinus über den 1. Johannesbrief* (Freiburg im Breisgau: Herder, 1940).

[7] Przywara, "St. Augustine and the Modern World," 280.

[8] Robert A. Krieg, *Romano Guardini: Proclaiming the Sacred In a Modern World* (Chicago: Archdiocese of Chicago Liturgy Training Publications, 1995), 16.

very basis" of Guardini's thought.[9] Guardini was also highly critical of the extrinsicist account of the relationship between nature and grace. In his 1939 work *Welt und Person*, which predated Henri de Lubac's *Surnaturel* by seven years, Guardini wrote: "Seen in the fullness of its energy as Paul proclaimed it and Augustine unfolded it, grace means something that is not added on to the nature of man for his perfection, but rather the form that man definitely is. Of course, this presupposes that we understand by the term 'man' what once again Paul and Augustine mean: not some being artificially let loose in a 'pure nature,' but rather that human being whom God intends and of whom Scripture speaks."[10]

In his later work *Freedom, Grace, and Destiny*, Guardini suggested that the ultimate character of the world is not "nature" but "history."[11] Since it proceeds from an act of God, nature exists *within* the world, a reality constructed in accordance with certain principles without consciousness or liberty that has to operate in conformity with these principles, but it is not synonymous with the world.[12] Moreover, Guardini wrote:

> The God of revelation is the same God who created the world and therefore the relation between revelation and the world is not merely one of difference. The Creator ordinated the world towards revelation, and this fundamental reality of existence has not been suppressed by sin. Scattered throughout the world are premonitions from which, in themselves, no single detail of revelation could be deduced but, once revelation has taken place, the Logos, as John declares, "without whom was made nothing that was made" comes "unto his own" and created being remains His property, even though it has turned against Him in sin and "His own received Him not" (John 1: 3–11). Thus a light is cast by revelation also on the things of the world. The paradox is in fact true that the real significance of these worldly things issues not from the things themselves but, in the first instance, from revelation.[13]

Alongside Guardini, another prominent teacher of the young Ratzinger was Gottlieb Söhngen (1892–1971). Söhngen was Professor of

---

[9] Hans Urs von Balthasar, *The Theology of Karl Barth* (San Francisco: Ignatius Press, 1992), 330.

[10] Romano Guardini, *Welt und Person* (Würzburg: Werkbund, 1939), 186–87.

[11] Romano Guardini, *Freedom, Grace, and Destiny* (London: Harvill, 1961), 120–21.

[12] Ibid., 121.

[13] Ibid., 101.

Fundamental Theology at the University of Munich and supervised both of Ratzinger's theses, the doctoral dissertation on Augustine's ecclesiology and the *Habilitationsschrift* on St. Bonaventure's theology of history. It was also under Söhngen that Ratzinger studied Newman's *Grammar of Assent*. Söhngen's rise to academic prominence was boosted by his publication of a two-volume work on the *analogia fidei* in 1934. These volumes were favorably reviewed by Karl Barth, although Barth doubted that Söhngen's approach was strongly representative of the Catholic position. It was a position that was more Augustinian in the priority it gave to faith than some of the more rationalist currents that Barth detected in the typical Catholic theology of the era. Ratzinger's former Prefect of Studies, Alfred Läpple, said of Söhngen:

> He usually never gave damning judgments on any author. He never refused a priori any contribution, from wherever it came. His method was to pick up and improve the good that could be found in any author and in every theological perspective, to weave the new things into the Tradition and then go ahead, indicating the further development that could follow. . . . In Söhngen Ratzinger also saw a willingness to rediscover Tradition understood as the theology of the Fathers. And a willingness to do theology by going back to the great sources: from Plato to Newman, via Thomas, Bonaventure, Luther, and obviously Saint Augustine.[14]

At Söhngen's funeral Ratzinger described his former teacher as "a radical and critical thinker" and a "radical believer."[15]

While Ratzinger was a student at the Theology Faculty in Munich, Läpple also introduced him to the works of Henri de Lubac, including his *Catholicism*, of which Ratzinger was later to write that it was perhaps de Lubac's most significant work. Ratzinger also described *Catholicism* as "a key reading event" that gave him "not only a new and deeper connection with the thought of the Fathers but also a new way of looking at theolo-

---

[14] Alfred Läpple, "That New Beginning That Bloomed among the Ruins," *30 Days*, no. 01/02, 2006, accessed March 8, 2017, http://www.30giorni.it/articoli_id_10125_l3.htm.

[15] Joseph Ratzinger, Beim Requiem in Köln am November 19, 1971: "Söhngen war ein radikal und kritisch Fragender. Auch heute kann man nicht radikaler fragen, als er es getan hat. Aber zugleich war er ein radikal Glaubender" (Pablo Blanco Sarto, *Joseph Ratzinger: Razon y Cristianismo: la Victoria de la inteligencia en el mundo de las religiones* [Madrid: Ediciones RIALP, 2005], 47).

gy and faith as such."[16] Following *Catholicism*, Ratzinger read de Lubac's *Corpus Mysticum*, which helped him to "enter into the required dialogue with Augustine."[17]

The significant point about this genealogy from Hofmann, through Pryzwara, Guardini, and Söhngen, to de Lubac is that not one of these authors who had engaged with the thought of St. Augustine in the first half of the twentieth century had neo-Manichean, Lutheran, or Calvinist inclinations or otherwise negative attitudes to the "world." Their fundamental dispositions were toward some form of Christian humanism, and they were all enlisting St. Augustine in this enterprise because of the value of his theological anthropology. Augustine wrestled with themes that were resurfacing among the early- to mid-twentieth-century existentialist philosophers. As Ratzinger has remarked, in the works of St. Augustine, "the passionate, suffering, questioning man is always right there, and one can identify with him."[18]

An extensive analysis of the various theological treatments of the concept of the "world" can be found in an essay by Cardinal Charles Journet entitled "Les trois cités: celle de Dieu, celle de l'homme, celle du diable."[19] Journet subdivides his presentation into treatments of the concept in the Old Testament, in the New Testament, and in the works of St. Augustine. In the section on the New Testament meanings, he cites Jacques Maritain's observation that the world cannot be neutral in relation to the Kingdom of God. Either the world aspires to be the Kingdom of God and is vivified by it, or it fights against it and exists in a relation of separation and of conflict.[20] The world is thus simultaneously an object of redemption and a city of evil. In his treatment of the concept in Augustine, Journet not only cites Augustine's comment in the *City of God* that the universe is more admirable than miracles but also draws attention to a lesser known statement from St. Augustine to the effect that the world is, for God, a kind of vast poem whose beauty unravels like a grandiose song. He also notes that one of St. Augustine's pastoral outreach audiences, the Donatists, did not want the world to include the Church. However, contrary to the Donatists, Au-

---

[16] Joseph Ratzinger, *Milestones: Memoirs 1927–1977* (San Francisco: Ignatius Press, 1998), 98.

[17] Ibid., 98.

[18] Joseph Ratzinger, *Salt of the Earth: The Church at the End of the Millennium—An Interview with Peter Seewald* (San Francisco: Ignatius Press, 1996), 61.

[19] Charles Journet, "Les trois cités: celle de Dieu, celle de l'homme, celle du diable," *Nova et Vetera* 33 (1958): 25–48.

[20] Jacques Maritain, *On the Philosophy of History* (New York: Scribner, 1957), 136.

gustine was of the view that to say that the world can be reconciled to God and saved by Christ is to say that the world means the Church, who alone, reconciled to God by Christ, is saved.[21] Journet sums up the position thus: "the damned world persecutes; the reconciled world is persecuted, it is the Church, *mundus damnatus, quidquid praeter Ecclesiam; mundus reconciliatus, Ecclesia.*"[22] With reference to the same phrase, Ernest Fortin, in his Saint Augustine Lecture of 1971, wrote, "The Church is not an entity distinct from the world but the world reconciled unto itself and unto God: *mundus reconciliatus ecclesia.*"[23]

This way of understanding the Church–world relationship is also evident in Balthasar's exegesis on Christ's words, "As the Father has sent me, so I send you into the world." Balthasar wrote: "As Christ fulfils the will of the Father precisely by going away from the Father and so remains one with the Father, so too the Church fulfils the will of Christ in her going into the world and so remains one with Him. Indeed, this 'going away' has its ultimate source and justification in the intra-divine 'going away' of the Son from the Father himself, in the eternal *missio* in which all missions in salvation history are rooted."[24]

As a consequence of this reading, Balthasar observed that the Church, in her being sent out to the world, "is herself fundamentally a part of the world, just as Christ as man was a part of the world."[25] Moreover, "the Church walks in the path of redemption by plunging with determination into the world and becoming herself the tool of this redemption, the *instrumentum redemptionis.*"[26]

The contrary tendency to think of the Church and the world dualistically has arisen apace with the emergence of the concept of the "secular" as a distinct ontological realm. Several authors have mapped this development, including Oliver O'Donovan and John Milbank. They both make the observation that, initially, the concept of the *saeculum* or secular order referred to time, not space: the *saeculum* was the time between Christ's res-

---

21   St. Augustine, *Ad donatistas post collationem* 8.11, cited in Journet, "Les trois cités," 44n4.

22   Charles Journet, "Les trois cités," 45.

23   Ernest Fortin, "Political Realism and Christianity in the Thought of St. Augustine," The Saint Augustine Lecture Series, 1971 (Philadelphia, PA: Villanova University Press, 1972), 25.

24   Hans Urs von Balthasar, "The Father, the Scholastics, and Ourselves," *Communio* 24 (Summer 1997): 347–96, at 362.

25   Ibid., 363.

26   Ibid.

urrection and return in glory and had nothing to do with social spheres.[27] S. Joel Garver has explained the notion in this manner: "Ecclesial order and civil order thus do not occupy two different spaces, but two different times: the Church having an eternal end, rooted in God's past saving acts in Christ, made present now in word and sacrament; the civil order having a temporal function within the present *saeculum*, ordained to continually pass away, though its treasures are carried in the bosom of the Church into the eternal kingdom."[28]

An Augustinian understanding of the relationship between the Church and the world such as it was expressed in Balthasar's exegesis above, however, did not provide the theological infrastructure for *Gaudium et Spes*. The infrastructure was the subject of much debate and the inevitable compromises that follow when there is little consensus about the best way to proceed. In his *Principles of Catholic Theology*, first published in 1982, Ratzinger lamented that, "despite many attempts to clarify it in section two of *Gaudium et Spes*, [the concept of the world] continues to be used in a pretheological stage":

> By "world" the Council means the counterpart of the Church. The purpose of the text is to bring the two into a relationship of cooperation, the goal of which is the "reconstruction of the 'world.'" The Church cooperates with the world in order to build up the world—it is thus that we might characterize the vision that informs the text. It is not clear, however, whether the world that cooperates and the world that is to be built up are one and same world; it is not clear what meaning is intended by the word "world" in every instance. In any event, we can be sure that the authors, who were aware that they spoke for the Church, acted on the assumption that they themselves were not the world but its counterpart and that they had up to then had a relationship to it that was, in fact, unsatisfactory where it existed at all. To that extent, we must admit, the text represents a kind of ghetto mentality. The Church is understood as a closed entity, but she is striving to remedy the situation. By "world," it would seem, the

---

27 Oliver O'Donovan, *The Desire of the Nations: Rediscovering the Roots of Political Theology* (Cambridge: Cambridge University Press, 1996); John Milbank, *Theology and Social Theory: Beyond Secular Reason* (Oxford: Blackwell, 1990).

28 S. Joel Garver, "There is another *King*: Gospel as Politics," accessed March 8, 2017, http://www.religiocity.org/2007/02/19/there-is-another-king-gospel-as-politics-by-joel-garver/.

document understands the whole scientific and technical reality of the present and all those who are responsible for it or who are at home in its mentality.[29]

Thus defined, the "world" comes across as a concept embracing all those social institutions in which the Church has little or no influence, and the document sounds like a plea from the ghetto to be offered the occasional invitation into the hallowed halls of secular academies. As E. Michael Jones remarked, the Council occurred at the high noon of the Catholic inferiority complex, at a moment in history when Catholic intellectuals, tired of being regarded as reactionary and anti-intellectual, "lusted after modernity."[30]

There was also a Church–humanity dualism operating within the Church–world dualism in *Gaudium et Spes*. Ratzinger lamented the use of the term *genus humanum* to refer to the Church's dialogue partner in the modern world. The Church herself, he claimed, is part of the *genus humanum* and cannot be contradistinguished from it:

> The Church meets its vis-à-vis in the human race. . . . But it cannot exclude itself from the human race and then artificially create a solidarity which in any case is the Church's lot. The lack of understanding shown in this matter by those who drafted the text can probably only be attributed to the deeply-rooted extrinsicism of ecclesiastical thought, to long acquaintance with the Church's exclusion from the general course of development and to a retreat into a special little ecclesiastical world from which an attempt is then made to speak to the rest of the world.[31]

At the foundation of the "deeply rooted extrinsicism" was a tendency to think of the Church canonically or bureaucratically, not mystically—to presume an ecclesiology based more on the Tridentine era theology than the multidimensional outlook one finds in de Lubac and Balthasar and upon which the post-conciliar "Communio" theology was built. Both de

---

[29] Joseph Ratzinger, *Principles of Catholic Theology* (San Francisco: Ignatius Press, 1987), 379–80.

[30] E. Michael Jones, *Living Machines: Bauhaus Architecture as Sexual Ideology* (San Francisco: Ignatius Press, 1995), 42.

[31] Joseph Ratzinger, "The Dignity of the Human Person," in *Commentary on the Documents of the Second Vatican Council*, vol. III, ed. Herbert Vorgrimler (London: Burns and Oates, 1969), 119.

Lubac and Balthasar tried to steer away from a narrowly juridical ecclesiology and instead presented the Church as a symphonic interplay of different spiritual missions and relationships. The relations within the Trinity were of primary importance, but also important were the typological relationships found in the Scriptures, and the sacramental and historical relationships between the Old and New Testaments.

With reference to the typographical relationships, de Lubac pointed out that the Church is at once Mount Zion (according to St. Basil), Noah's Ark (according to St. Augustine), the paradise in the midst of which Christ, the Tree of Life, is planted (according St. Irenaeus), a foreigner, a slave, and even a harlot. On the one hand, we see "an assembly of sinners, a mixed herd, wheat gathered with the straw, . . . on the other, the unspotted virgin, mother of saints, born on Calvary from the pierced side of Christ."[32]

In his treatment of typology, Balthasar referred to a "Christological constellation" of characters, each representing a different spiritual mission in the life of the Church. For example, the Johannine mission (typified by St. John) is one of contemplative love and prayer; the Jacobite mission (typified by St. James) is one of preserving the tradition uncorrupted; the Petrine mission (typified by St. Peter) is one of ecclesial governance; and the Pauline mission (typified by St. Paul) is one of prophetic movement and utterance. Each mission is dependent on the others and operates within a symphonic harmony.

The conclusion to be drawn from this *Communio* ecclesiology, which Ratzinger has long argued was one of the great advances of the Second Vatican Council, is that any assessment of the relationship between the Church and the world requires something more theologically complex than a merely juridical understanding of the Church and a merely sociological understanding of the world. However, in the early years of the 1960s, the *Communio* ecclesiology was still in its infancy and those responsible for drafting *Gaudium et Spes* struggled to articulate a coherent analytical framework for a subject as large and complex as the Church's relationship to the world.

In his introduction to his commentary on *Gaudium et Spes* published in 1969, Ratzinger noted that §2 of the Zurich text of the document had attempted to justify the whole notion of the Church's dialogue with "the world" by means of the scriptural reference to reading the signs of the times (Matt 16:3 and Luke 12:56). This earlier draft regarded epochs as

---

[32] Henri de Lubac, *Catholicism and the Common Destiny of Man*, 69.

a sign and a voice to the extent that it involves God's presence or absence; and consequently it was argued that the voice of the age must be regarded as the voice of God. However, Ratzinger observed that this idea was, quite correctly, criticized: "To link the Roman proverb on time as the voice of God with Jesus's eschatological warning against the blindness of his nation which, though on the look-out for signs, was not able to interpret him, God's eschatological sign to that age, or his message, was considered not only exegetically unacceptable but of doubtful validity in itself. Since Christ is the real 'sign of the time,' is he not the actual antithesis to the authority of *chronos* expressed in the proverb '*vox temporis vox Dei*?'"[33]

The ideas that Christ is the "sign of the time" and the "light of the nations," and thus that the conciliar documents should be read with a Christocentric accent, was not, however, the dominant reading of the documents in the 1960s. Instead, the central message of the Council was often taken to be a general "openness to the world," however defined. This openness was then taken up by the correlationist theologians, of whom Edward Schillebeeckx was the most prominent, who sought to correlate the faith to the culture of the times. The correlationists also gave priority to the first sections of *Gaudium et Spes*, which were addressed to people of goodwill, or "the world" at large. Walter Kasper and others have noted that there is a tension between the first sections of the document, which are merely theistically hued and were directed to all peoples of goodwill regardless of faith traditions, and the later sections, which foster a Christocentric Trinitarian anthropology and thereby presuppose belief in Christian revelation.[34]

Ratzinger agrees with Kasper that a major problem with *Gaudium et Spes* is that those responsible for its drafting never resolved the inherent tension between a merely theistically hued account of the human person and an explicitly Trinitarian account. The Trinitarian account, he said, "fell victim to the tendency to simplify."[35] Speaking directly on the treatment of the human person in §12, Ratzinger complained that "there was not a radical enough rejection of a doctrine of man divided into philosophy and theology." The text was "still based on a schematic representation of nature and the supernatural viewed far too much as merely juxtaposed." To the mind of the critics of §12, it "took as its starting-point the fiction

---

[33] Ratzinger, "The Dignity of the Human Person," 115.

[34] Walter Kasper, "The Theological Anthropology of *Gaudium et Spes*," *Communio* 23 (1996): 129–40; and David L. Schindler, "Christology and the Imago Dei: Interpreting *Gaudium et Spes*," *Communio* 23 (1996): 156–84.

[35] Ratzinger, "The Dignity of the Human Person," 116.

that it is possible to construct a rational philosophical picture of man intelligible to all and on which all men of goodwill can agree, the actual Christian doctrines being added to this as a sort of crowning conclusion. The latter then tends to appear as a sort of special possession of Christians, which others ought not to make a bone of contention but which at bottom can be ignored."[36] This approach thereby prompted the question of "why exactly the reasonable and perfectly free human being described in the first articles was suddenly burdened with the story of Christ."[37] Ratzinger went on to say that this criticism (the idea that the earlier sections of *Gaudium et Spes* seem to imply that the later sections are a mere optional extra for Catholics who want to take it) was the basis of the protest against the "optimism" of the schema, not some "pessimistic view of man" or "an exaggerated theology of sin" more typically Lutheran than Catholic.[38]

At the end of this analysis Ratzinger noted that at the foundation of the conundrum was not only the relationship between nature and supernature but the relationship between faith and understanding. He was then critical of the habit of positing a strong division between philosophy and theology, a habit he associated with the Thomist tradition, though without naming any particular branches of the tradition or acknowledging the internal debates within that tradition that had, for example, flared in French Thomist circles in the 1930s.[39] He merely concluded that the juxtaposition had gradually been established but "no longer appears adequate" and that "there is, and must be, a human reason in faith; yet, conversely, every human reason is conditioned by a historical standpoint so that reason pure and simple does not exist."[40] In other words, he was critical of the tendency to read "reason" as Kantian reason.

Lest this statement be discredited as the "low point" of Ratzinger's "theological teenager" period, he reiterated his stance against "pure rea-

---

[36] Ibid., 119.

[37] Ibid., 120.

[38] Ibid.

[39] For an account of these debates, see *Reason Fulfilled by Revelation: The 1930s Christian Philosophy Debates in France*, ed. Gregory B. Sadler (Washington, DC: Catholic University of America Press, 2011). This book sets out the players in the 1930s Christian Philosophy debates in France and places them into the categories of: neo-Thomist opponents of Christian philosophy, Thomist proponents of Christian philosophy, and non-Thomist proponents of Christian philosophy. For a more general account of the different approaches to the relationship between faith and reason in the Thomist tradition that is not restricted to the French contributions to the debate, see Fergus Kerr, *After Aquinas: Versions of Thomism* (Oxford: Blackwell, 2002).

[40] Ratzinger, "The Dignity of the Human Person," 120.

son" in his 1996 address to the bishops of Mexico. In that address, he said that "neo-scholastic rationalism failed in its attempts to reconstruct the *preambula fidei* with wholly independent reasoning, with pure rational certainty."[41] Karl Barth, he said, was right to "reject philosophy as the foundation of faith, independent of faith," since, if that were so, "our faith would be dependent from the beginning to the end on changing philosophical theories."[42] Nonetheless, he rejected Barth's idea of faith as a pure paradox that can exist only against reason and totally independent of it.

As Aidan Nichols has argued, Ratzinger/Benedict's account of the faith and reason relationship sounds "highly Gilsonian" (according to whom the relationship is intrinsic) and "made *some* movement towards *bautainisme*, which, owing to its inheritance from traditionalism, considered faith to be an indispensable auxiliary to reason if reason were ever to attain fundamental truths."[43] Nichols also draws attention to affinities between Ratzinger's account of the faith and reason relationship and those of Franz Jacob Clemens and Paul Tillich. In general, Nichols observes that Benedict tends to unite "philosophy and theology in a single, internally differentiated but also internally cohesive, intellectual act" and, thus, what one finds in Benedict's many publications is a "convergence of the mainly philosophical disclosure of logos with the chiefly theological revelation of love."[44] "Love and Reason," Benedict writes, are the "twin pillars" of reality. This, in turn, gives rise to a quintessentially Augustinian theological anthropology that pays equal attention to the head and the heart, to objectivity and affectivity. As Paige E. Hochschild observes in *Memory in Augustine's Theological Anthropology*, for St. Augustine, "the two problems of knowledge and love cannot be separated, given that one determines the object for the other."[45]

At the time of the drafting of *Gaudium et Spes*, however, there was still a strong habit of thinking of faith and reason extrinsically. This was due, at least in part, to the influence of the first paragraph of chapter II of the First Vatican Council's *Dei Filius*. The much quoted "anathema" sentence reads: "If anyone says that the one, true God, our creator and lord,

---

[41] Joseph Ratzinger, "The Current Situation of Faith and Theology," *L'Osservatore Romano*, November 6, 1996, 4–6, at 6.

[42] Ibid., 6.

[43] Aidan Nichols, *Faith and Reason: From Hermes to Benedict XVI* (Leominster, UK: Gracewing, 2009), 228–30.

[44] Ibid., 228 and 193.

[45] Paige E. Hochschild, *Memory in Augustine's Theological Anthropology* (Oxford: Oxford University Press, 2012), 139.

cannot be known with certainty from the things that have been made, by the natural light of human reason, let him be anathema."[46] That particular paragraph was drafted at a moment in time when the Church was under attack from rationalist philosophers and, thus, when her champions were focused on defending the rationality of the faith. Precisely how it is to be interpreted in the light of later debates and magisterial documents, especially the "Catholic philosophy" debates of the 1930s, the conciliar document *Dei Verbum*, and Pope John Paul II's *Fides et Ratio*, remains a subject of academic dispute.[47] Fergus Kerr has noted that "it remained unsettled at Vatican I whether the natural light by which reason can attain knowledge of God should be equated with the prelapsarian light enjoyed by Adam in the Garden of Eden or the light in which someone in a state of grace might exercise his reasoning powers, or the light which someone might supposedly have independently of the effects of sin and grace."[48]

Moreover, Kerr observes that, while the First Vatican Council (1869–1870) decreed that, for Catholics, it is a dogma of faith that we can have certain knowledge of God by the natural light of reason, it was only in the Anti-Modernist Oath (1910) that this knowledge was defined as rationally demonstrable by cosmological arguments. Similarly, Noel O'Sullivan has suggested that what is interesting about *Dei Filius* is not so much what it says but rather what it does not say, and in particular, "one is struck by the absence of a Trinitarian dimension in the definition of 1870."[49] In a manner that is consonant with Ratzinger's criticisms, O'Sullivan observes:

> The key difficulty that arises from this overly rationalistic approach is that a separation arises between creation and salvation. In this perspective creation is seen as primarily concerned with the world and the universe, while the human being is only considered on a secondary level, as a being in the world. The human is treated as of primary concern only in the context of salvation. The act of creation is antecedent to humanity and is of no significance where revelation and salvation history is concerned. Creation is

---

[46] *Decrees of the Ecumenical Councils*, ed. and trans. Norman P. Tanner (London: Sheed and Ward, 1990).

[47] Fergus Kerr, "Knowing God by Reason Alone: What Vatican I Never Said," *New Black-friars* 91, no. 1033 (May 2010): 215–28, at 222.

[48] Kerr, "Knowing God by Reason Alone," 222.

[49] Noel O'Sullivan, *Christ and Creation: Christology as the Key to Interpreting the Theology of Creation in the Works of Henri de Lubac* (Oxford: Peter Lang, 2009), 139.

just a neutral shell where salvation history is acted out. Even God is looked on differently, depending on whether the perspective is that of creation or salvation. From the perspective of creation taken in isolation, God is the first cause of everything that exists: there is an immensurable gap between Creator and creature. From the perspective of salvation alone, God is a personal being in relationship with humanity. As a result of this manner of viewing creation and salvation in such distinct categories, an opposition between faith and reason develops. Faith is seen as concerned with the salvific action of God and not connected to the creative action of God.[50]

On Ratzinger's reading, §21 of *Gaudium et Spes* represents a kind of immature compromise between the rationalist interpretation of *Dei Filius* and some of the criticisms of extrinsicism that began in the works of Maurice Blondel and flowed into the French Thomist debates in the 1940s. Thus he wrote:

> The term "*ratio*" was simply meant to recall in abbreviated form the well-known definitions of Vatican I, and by the addition or retention of "*experientia*" the aim was to limit the neo-scholastic rationalism contained in the formula of 1870 and to place its over-static idea of "*ratio naturalis*" in a more historical perspective. The text indicates . . . that the possibilities of reason in regard to knowledge of God should be thought of less in the form of a non-historical syllogism of the *philosophia perennis* than simply as the concrete fact that man throughout his whole history has known himself confronted with God and consequently in virtue of his own history finds himself in relation with God as an inescapable feature of his own existence.[51]

The Conciliar document that dealt with these issues more to Ratzinger's liking was *Dei Verbum*. As Gregory Baum has argued, while *Dei Filius* did not address the issue of *how* knowledge of the true God based on human reason is related to the saving actions of God revealed in Christ, the "profounder understanding of revelation" offered by *Dei Verbum* "in-

---

[50] Ibid., 139–40.
[51] Ratzinger, "The Dignity of the Human Person," 153.

troduces a new theological epistemology."[52] Baum summarizes this epistemology in the following paragraph:

> Vatican I affirms that "God, the beginning and end of all things, can be known with certainty from created reality by the light of human reason." In accordance with Vatican II, we can now say that if God allows Himself to be found—across whatever distance—through the works of His creation as understood by human reason, this does not take place because of an independent or sovereign act of man, but rather because of the appeal which the gracious God through His creation makes to the mind and heart of men. The "natural" knowledge of God is related to the history of salvation appointed for the whole human family, which is revealed once and for all in Jesus Christ.[53]

In short, *Dei Verbum* emphasizes that the structure of revelation is Trinitarian, and this "profounder understanding" is something of a solvent for rationalist interpretations of *Dei Filius*. This deeper theological epistemology was not, however, integrated into *Gaudium et Spes*, and notwithstanding the addition of the concept of *experientia*, which was a move in an antirationalist direction, Ratzinger regarded §21 of the pastoral constitution as an inadequate response to atheism. He suggested that, in order to address the concerns of atheists, God's invisibility is something that has to be taken into account:

> [Christianity] cannot be taken seriously if it acts as if reason and revelation present a smooth, plain certainty accessible to everyone; in that case atheism could only be a matter of evil will. In that case, too, the atheist could not consider that he was being taken seriously. He would feel little inclination to engage in discussion when his cause is declared from the start to be contrary to plain reason and he is treated merely as a sick man worthy of pity, the causes of whose malady are being inquired into so that he may be cured.[54]

---

[52] Gregory Baum, "Vatican II's Constitution on Revelation: History and Interpretation," *Theological Studies* 28, no. 1 (March 9, 1967): 51–75, at 62.

[53] Ibid., 64.

[54] Ratzinger, "The Dignity of the Human Person," 154–55.

Taken as a whole, Ratzinger regarded §21 as offering no advance in regard to the problem raised at Vatican I. He thought the mere addition of *experientia* to *ratio* would not solve the problems and that the whole article fails to engage with contemporary theological reflections, especially those fostered by Karl Barth's criticisms of the doctrine of the *analogia entis*:

> The Council passed over the essentials of the *theologia negativa*. It took no account of Augustine's epistemology, which is much deeper than that of Aquinas, for it is well aware that the organ by which God can be seen cannot be a non-historical "ratio naturalis" which just does not exist, but only the *ratio pura*, i.e. *purificata* or, as Augustine expresses it echoing the gospel, the *cor purum* ("Blessed are the pure in heart, for they shall see God"). Augustine also knows that the necessary purification of sight takes place through faith (Acts 15:9) and through love, at all events not as a result of reflection alone and not at all by man's own power. By ignoring these approaches, the opportunity was lost of manifesting the positive service to faith performed by atheism.[55]

Against Barth, however, Ratzinger applauded the fact that §21 does at least emphasize that faith "cannot remain inaccessible to a reason which is ready to listen."[56] Ratzinger is not a Barthian, but he shares Barth's aversion to rationalism and his linkage of rationalism with secularism.

Notwithstanding his specific judgments about the inadequacy of the conciliar engagement with the phenomenon of atheism, Ratzinger nonetheless approved of the general orientation of a small subcommission consisting of Cardinal König, Cardinal Šeper, Henri de Lubac, and Jean Daniélou that decided to deal with the question of atheism as an anthropological (not a narrowly epistemological) issue. These committee members understood that atheism "does not simply express a metaphysical failure or a breakdown in epistemology, but draws its inspiration from an authentic desire for a true humanism."[57] Further, Ratzinger asserted that "Atheism is a question which can only be understood on the level of existence; a philosophy of pure essences cannot cope with it."[58] He formu-

---

[55] Ibid., 155.
[56] Ibid.
[57] Ibid., 146.
[58] Ibid.

lated the fundamental issue thus: Is God merely a projection of man, or is it God who makes it possible for man to be human?[59]

The language used by Ratzinger for describing how to combat atheism was that of "showing the face of God to the world." This, he said, has nothing to do with a "one-sided activism." Rather, an important component of it is "participation in the spirituality of the Cross," and indeed, Ratzinger noted that martyrdom is the clearest exposition of the face of God. He concluded: "The real answer to atheism is the life of the Church, which must manifest the face of God by showing its own face of unity and love. Conversely this includes the admission that the disunity of Christians and their consent to systems of social injustice, hide the face of God. It also implies the realization that knowing God is not a question of pure reason alone, that there is an obscuration of God in the world produced by guilt, which can only be removed by penance and conversion."[60]

Reading this passage in the first week of Lent, 2013, the final week of the pontificate of Benedict XVI, when this essay was first written, was quite a sobering exercise. One senses that Ratzinger/Benedict's decision to resign from the papacy represents an exchange of a Petrine mission for a Johannine mission. Jean Daniélou, one of those *periti* Ratzinger praised for understanding that atheism is fundamentally an anthropological rather than epistemological issue (although he would no doubt agree that there is an epistemological dimension to the anthropological problem), wrote the following words: "Our Lord has told us that souls are to be won away from the Devil first by fasting and vigils, and that the great battle is fought in the heart of the desert, in the depth of solitude, on the summit of Carmel, before it is fought through the ministry of preachers, on the great highways and in the villages. . . . We must tear souls away from Satan first of all through prayer, penance and sacrifice."[61] Just as John Paul II died on the stage of the world bearing witness to a Christian understanding of death with dignity, Benedict XVI left the stage of the world bearing witness to the truth that prayer and fasting are sometimes the only way to triumph over extreme evil.

A core element of any anthropology is its understanding of freedom. Here it is highly significant that, of all Ratzinger's criticisms of *Gaudium et Spes*, his most acidic comments are directed against the treatment of

---

[59] Ibid.

[60] Ibid., 157.

[61] Jean Daniélou, *The Salvation of the Nations*, trans. Angeline Bouchard (New York: Sheed and Ward, 1950), 43.

freedom in §17: it was "one of the least satisfactory of the whole document"; it "cannot stand up to either theological or philosophical criticism"; philosophically, "it by-passes the whole modern discussion of freedom"; it "shut itself out from the factual situation of man whose freedom only comes into effect through a lattice of determining factors"; "theologically speaking it leaves aside the whole complex of problems which Luther, with polemical one-sidedness, comprised in the term *servum arbitrium*." Moreover, "the whole text gives scarcely a hint of the discord which runs through man and which is described so dramatically in Rom 7:13–25. It even falls into downright Pelagian terminology when it speaks of man *'sese ab omni passionum captivitate liberans finem suum persequitur et apta subsidia . . . procurat.'*"[62] He concluded:

> If optimism in John XXIII's sense means readiness for today and tomorrow, if it means abandoning nostalgia for the past for a spirituality of hope in the midst of each particular present moment, then it does not in any way impose the platitudes of an ethics modeled on that of the Stoa. Here it would have been possible to learn from Marxism about the extent of human alienation and decadence. Not to take them seriously does not mean to think highly of man, but to deceive him about the gravity of his situation.[63]

Positively, however, Ratzinger noted that the Council fathers were keen to affirm man's freedom against the variety of determinisms that characterized early-twentieth-century history. Although no specific examples were given, the racist determinism of the Nazi ideology, the class determinism of the Marxist ideology, and the hormonal or sex-drive determinism of Freudian psychology were all likely to have been in their thoughts.

While the Council fathers may have been so focused on rejecting these various determinisms that they failed to analyze in any depth the limitations on human freedom, the whole pontificate of John Paul II can be read as a theo-dramatic study on this very topic. Against the backdrop of the Cold War, many of John Paul II's publications dealt with critiques of liberal Pelagian conceptions of freedom, on the one side, and Marxist conceptions on the other. As he remarked in an address to the scholars of Lublin University in 1987 in the dying days of the Communist regime, "the human person must stave off a double-temptation: the temptation to

---

[62] Ratzinger, "The Dignity of the Human Person," 138.
[63] Ibid.

make the truth about himself subordinate to his freedom and the temptation to subordinate himself to the world of objects: he has to refuse to succumb to the temptation of both self-idolatry and of self-subjectification."[64] The first temptation is the liberal temptation; the second is the Marxist. Both are erroneous because, as he was later to express the problem poetically, "the human person is a pillar that has a crack to be sealed within."[65] Only grace can seal the crack, and grace is not part of the conceptual framework of the liberal or the Marxist.

In addition to the lack of clarity regarding the relationship of anthropology to Christology, or more specifically, of a merely theistically colored account of creation to an explicitly Trinitarian account, there is the further problem of the interpretation of §36 of *Gaudium et Spes*. This paragraph speaks of a *terrenarum rerum autonomia*, which is normally rendered in English (including in the official Holy See English translation) as "the legitimate autonomy of earthly affairs." With reference to this particular phrase David L. Schindler has argued that "the root meaning of the '*legitima autonomia*' finds its proper meaning in an analogy of being based on the descent of God into the world," and further, that "the organic relation between the Trinity and the creature established in Jesus Christ does not reduce creaturely autonomy but rather grants it a new and expanded meaning."[66] The paragraph is capable of a nonsecularizing interpretation, especially if it is read by persons who have studied theology. However, a "plain person" reading the phrase "a legitimate autonomy of earthly affairs" is likely to interpret the expression quite differently from a professional theologian.

Cardinal Angelo Scola has noted that there is a "latent ambiguity" around the interpretation of the principle of the autonomy of earthly affairs.[67] Scola reads §36 as an acknowledgement that there is a realm of life that is the responsibility of the laity. He does not read it as authority for the proposition that there might be aspects of life that have no intrinsic relationship to the Creator and, thus, that there might be social provinces in which theological insight has nothing to contribute.

---

[64] Pope John Paul II, "Address to the Scholars of Lublin University," *Christian Life in Poland*, November 1987, 51.

[65] See the poem *La Libertá*, written by John Paul II and recorded as a song by Placido Domingo.

[66] David L. Schindler, "Trinity, Creation and the Order of Intelligence in the Modern Academy," *Communio* 28 (Fall 2001): 406–29, at 407.

[67] Angelo Scola, "El Peligro de una Falsa 'Autonomia,'" *Humanitas: Revista de Antropologica y Cultura Christianas* 66 (Fall 2012): 296–301, at 299.

Consistent with such an interpretation, in an essay on the contributions of Cardinal Joseph Frings to the conciliar debates, Ratzinger drew attention to Frings's speech of October 27, 1964, in which he warned that earthly advances do not transfer directly to the Kingdom of God. As Ratzinger expressed his argument:

> The three stages of creation, incarnation, and Passover must be seen each in their dynamic relation, each with its own weight and each in relation to the others. Literally, his [Frings's] formulation was, "For the Christian life in the world three revealed truths are always to be kept before us: creation, which teaches us to love the things of the world as God's work; the Incarnation, which spurs us on to dedicate to God all the things of the world; cross and resurrection, which leads us in the imitation of Christ to sacrifice and continence with regard to the things of the world."[68]

What Scola identified as a latent ambiguity in *Gaudium et Spes* §36 may be identified as a concrete example of the problems that arise when interpreters of the conciliar documents approach them with a lopsided focus on creation at the expense of the Incarnation and Paschal mysteries.

In addition to all these various problems of interpretation relating to theological anthropology and the Church–world relationship, there is the problem (more of a linguistic and sociological nature) that, although there are many references to the modern world and modern man to be found in *Gaudium et Spes*, at the time of the document's drafting by predominately Francophone theologians, there was very little scholarship available on "modernity as a cultural formation" (aside from a few scattered works in German and English). The Canadian philosopher Kenneth Schmitz has remarked that, in the 1960s, very few Catholic scholars had any understanding of what sociologists now mean by the concept of modernity: "Had we been more perceptive we might have guessed that the foundations of modernity were beginning to crack under an increasingly incisive attack. But we had no such cultural concept as modernity: all we had instead was the historical category: modern philosophy."[69]

In his autobiographical work *A Theologian's Journey*, Thomas F.

---

[68] Joseph Ratzinger, "Cardinal Frings's Speeches during the Second Vatican Council: Apropos of A. Muggeridge's *The Desolate City*," *Communio* 15 (1988): 131–47, at 143–44.

[69] Kenneth L. Schmitz, "Postmodernism and the Catholic Tradition," *American Catholic Philosophical Quarterly* 73, no. 2 (1999): 223–53, at 235.

O'Meara suggested that much conflict would have been avoided if Romano Guardini's perspectives on modernity had been read by the Council fathers.[70] That they were not was probably due to the narrowness of the seminary curricula of the time in which many of the Fathers were formed. Preconciliar seminary curricula were not designed for the kind of interdisciplinary analysis that now goes by the label of the "theology of culture." Preconciliar theology prided itself on being "above history," not on its intellectual analysis of transient historical-cultural phenomena. It is striking that those Catholic scholars who were interested in modernity as a cultural formation were predominately members of the laity, for example, Georges Bernanos and Christopher Dawson.

Today however, some five decades later, most post-conciliar-generation scholars are familiar with the many critiques of modernity from theological and sociological perspectives. There is, for example, Alasdair MacIntyre's reading of modernity as the severance of the classical–theistic synthesis, Charles Taylor's reading as a mutation of the same synthesis, Hans Blumenberg's reading of it as the re-occupation of defunct Christian concepts by a new non-Christian substance, Eric Voegelin's thesis of it as neo-gnosticism, and the "radical orthodoxy" reading represented by Catherine Pickstock and John Milbank, as the heretical reconstruction of the classical–theistic synthesis. Regardless of the differences in nuance between severance, mutation, re-occupation, neo-gnosticism, and heretical reconstruction, in each of these accounts of the culture of modernity there is a common agreement that this culture developed in opposition to the medieval theological (especially Thomistic) synthesis and the culture that embodied its principles. Theologians such as Balthasar would add that the severance of the relationships among the true, the beautiful, and the good was a central pathological feature of the new culture.

Tragically, in the 1960s and beyond, Catholic theologians who interpreted the Council, especially *Gaudium et Spes*, as a call to make the Catholic faith more compatible with the culture of modernity were often unaware of just how far behind the times such thinking really was. Augustine Di Noia has noted: "The Post-Conciliar interpretation of John XXIII's vision of *aggiornamento* as updating theology is, from the perspective of post-modern eyes, a project which has never really caught up, while conceived more grandly as modernization, it is already far behind."[71]

---

[70] Thomas F. O'Meara, *A Theologian's Journey* (Boston: Paulist Press, 2002), 218.

[71] Augustine Di Noia, "American Catholic Theology at Century's End: Postconciliar, Postmodern and Post-Thomistic," *The Thomist* 54 (1990): 499–518, at 518.

Both St. John Paul II and Benedict XVI emphasized the Christo-centric sections of *Gaudium et Spes*, in particular §22, as a remedy to the correlationist interpretations of the document that often resulted in the teachings of the Church being expressed in the language of liberal modernity and that today, in our postmodern times, now sound so dated as to be almost incomprehensible to those born after the 1970s. By making §22 the hermeneutical lens through which the rest of the document is read, many of the problems that Ratzinger, Kasper, Scola, and others identified can be overcome. Ratzinger has suggested that the merit of *Gaudium et Spes*, notwithstanding its unresolved inner tensions and tendency to use ambiguous language, is that it offered a "daring new theological anthropology," albeit one that was not well expressed in the actual document. As he wrote:

> Article 22 thus returns to the starting-point, Article 12, and presents Christ as the eschatological Adam to whom the first Adam already pointed; as the true image of God which transforms man once more into likeness to God. The attempt to pursue discussion with non-believers on the basis of the idea of "*humanitas*," here culminates in the endeavor to interpret being human Christologically and so attain the "*resolutio in theologiam*" which, it is true, also means "*resolutio in hominem*" (provided the sense of "*homo*" is understood deeply enough). We are probably justified in saying that here for the first time in an official document of the magisterium, a new type of completely Christocentric theology appears.[72]

And he continues slightly further on:

> In Article 22 the idea of the "*assumption hominis*" is first touched upon in its full ontological depth. The human nature of all men is one; Christ's taking to himself the one human nature of man is an event which affects every human being; consequently human nature in every human being is henceforward Christologically characterized. . . . This outlook is probably also important because it opens a bridge between the theology of the incarnation and that of the cross. A theology of the incarnation situated too much on the level of essence, may be tempted to be satisfied with the ontological phenomenon: God's being and man's have been conjoined. . . . But since it is made clear that man's being is not that of a pure

---

[72] Ratzinger, "The Dignity of the Human Person," 159.

essence, and that he only attains his reality by his activity, it is at once evident that we cannot rest content with a purely essentialist outlook. Man's being must therefore be examined precisely in its activities.[73]

Herein lies an important point of convergence between Ratzinger/Benedict and Wojtyła/John Paul II. They are both interested in relationality or that dimension of the human person that is determined by their relations with other persons, including each of the Persons of the Trinity, in time and history. Schmaus expressed the principle thus: "Nature cannot come to its fulfilment in the antechambers of God's love and glory, but only in the inner chamber of his Trinitarian divine life."[74] Michael Hanby made the same point in his *Augustine and Modernity* when he wrote that at issue within the culture of modernity is the Trinity itself, specifically whether the meaning of human nature and human agency are understood to occur *within* Christ's mediation of the love and delight shared as *donum* between the Father and the Son, or beyond it.[75]

Among Benedict's many papal homilies and documents, one can find numerous criticisms of the culture of modernity from a Christocentric Trinitarian perspective. One of the most sustained criticisms is found in his second encyclical, *Spe Salvi*, which some commentators have described as his "antidote" to the secularist renderings of poorly drafted passages in *Gaudium et Spes*. Although this is probably an accident (not something he intended), §22 of *Spe Salvi* resonates strongly with the Christocentricism of §22 of *Gaudium et Spes*. Here he wrote:

> A self-critique of modernity is needed in dialogue with Christianity and its concept of hope. In this dialogue Christians too, in the context of their knowledge and experience, must learn anew in what their hope truly consists, what they have to offer to the world and what they cannot offer. Flowing into this self-critique of the modern age there also has to be a self-critique of modern Christianity, which must constantly renew its self-understanding setting out from its roots. On this subject, all we can attempt here are a few brief observations. First we must ask ourselves: what does "progress" really mean; what does it promise and what does

---

[73] Ibid., 160.

[74] Schmaus, *Katholische Dogmatik*, 2:200.

[75] Michael Hanby, *Augustine and Modernity* (London: Routledge, 2003), 73.

it not promise? . . . If technical progress is not matched by corresponding progress in man's ethical formation, in man's inner growth (cf. *Eph* 3:16; *2 Cor* 4:16), then it is not progress at all, but a threat for man and for the world.

In the following paragraph, he was critical of notions of rationality "detached from God" and he argued that "if progress, in order to be progress, needs moral growth on the part of humanity, then the reason behind action and capacity for action is likewise urgently in need of integration through reason's openness to the saving forces of faith, to the differentiation between good and evil. Only thus does reason become truly human."

This means that the great Enlightenment project—severing faith from reason and then, with a much reduced rational capacity, setting about building political utopias based on nothing more than this faith-less rationality—was not going to foster the very freedom it desired. Hence, there is Benedict's judgment in *Spe Salvi* §24 that "the right state of human affairs, the moral well-being of the world can never be guaranteed simply through structures alone, however good they are":

> Since man always remains free and since his freedom is always fragile, the kingdom of good will never be definitively established in this world. Anyone who promises the better world that is guaranteed to last forever is making a false promise; he is overlooking human freedom. Freedom must constantly be won over for the cause of good. Free assent to the good never exists simply by itself. If there were structures which could irrevocably guarantee a determined—good—state of the world, man's freedom would be denied, and hence they would not be good structures at all.

In particular, in §25 of *Spe Salvi*, Benedict concluded that Francis Bacon and those who followed in the intellectual current of modernity that he inspired were wrong to believe that man would be redeemed through science.

Nothing in these paragraphs however should be construed as a Christian call to withdraw from the world. Earlier in *Spe Salvi*, at §15, Benedict explicitly rejected the idea that the Church's endorsement of the monastic vocation has something to do with a "contempt for the world" mentality. He suggested that, if we take "a more or less randomly chosen episode from the Middle Ages," the monastic movement of St. Bernard of Clairvaux, St. Bernard was not encouraging youth to treat monasteries "as places of flight from the world (*contemptus mundi*) and of withdrawal from responsibility for the world, in search of private salvation." Rather, St. Bernard's monks were performing "a task for the whole Church and hence also for the world." In the later paragraphs of *Spe Salvi* (§§34–36), Benedict exhorted Catholics to "keep the world open to God":

> We can open ourselves and the world and allow God to enter: we can open ourselves to truth, to love, to what is good. This is what the saints did, those who, as "God's fellow workers," contributed to the world's salvation (cf. *1 Cor* 3:9; *1 Th* 3:2). We can free our life and the world from the poisons and contaminations that could destroy the present and the future. We can uncover the sources of creation and keep them unsullied, and in this way we can make a right use of creation, which comes to us as a gift, according to its intrinsic requirements and ultimate purpose.
>
> We know that this God exists, and hence that this power to "take away the sin of the world" (*Jn* 1:29) is present in the world. Through faith in the existence of this power, hope for the world's healing has emerged in history.

In the final analysis, the conflict over the correct interpretation of the Church's relationship to the world is not between grace sniffers and heresy sniffers or between those who want to plunder the spoils of the Egyptians (the "open to the world" types) and those who want nothing whatsoever to do with Egyptians (the "closed to the world" types). Rather, it is between those who think that human nature can or cannot come to fulfilment in the antechambers of God's love and glory. Ratzinger's Augustinianism was not a neo-Protestant Augustinianism fixated on the theology of the Cross, but instead a classically Catholic Christocentric Trinitarian Augustinianism for which the Incarnation is the fulcrum of history, one that presupposes creation and looks forward to the final renewal of the cosmos.

CHAPTER 3

Augustinian and Thomist Engagements with the World[1]

IN A REVIEW OF John L. Allen's biography *Cardinal Ratzinger: The Vatican's Enforcer*, the reviewer explained that Ratzinger's reservations about some aspects of *Gaudium et Spes* are "associated with his choice of Augustine as his principal theological guide" and, further, that "the divergence of views between John Paul II (a follower of Aquinas) and Joseph Ratzinger (a follower of Augustine) is profound."[2] This explanation is consistent with a common interpretation of the Augustinian tradition as having almost nothing to contribute to the Church's social teaching aside from just war theory and as regarding this world as merely a valley of tears, or at best, a strict academy for the practice of virtue, with its political orders being one of the many unfortunate consequences of original sin to be stoically endured.[3] According to the common caricature, Augustinians want to

---

[1]   First published in *American Catholic Philosophical Quarterly* 83 (Summer 2009): 441–61.

[2]   John Thornhill, "Vatican II Challenged the Church to Leave Its Tidy 'World Apart': The 'Open Church' of Vatican II," *Catalyst for Renewal* (Archives/Vatican-II/18-John-Thornhill), accessed March 9, 2017, http://www.catalyst-for-renewal.com.au/index.php?option=com_content&view=article&id=185&catid=16:archive-vatican-ii&Itemid=102. See also Joseph Ratzinger, "Der Weltdienst der Kirche: Auswirkungen von Gaudium et spes im letzten Jahrzehnt," in *Zehn Jahre Vaticanum II*, ed. M. Seybold (Regensburg: Pustet, 1976).

[3]   A list of key sources, by no means exhaustive, would include: Peter D. Barthory, *Political Theory as Public Confession: the Social and Political Theory of St. Augustine of Hippo* (New Brunswick, NJ: Transaction, 1981); Vernon J. Bourke, "The City of God and the Christian View of History," in *Wisdom from St. Augustine* (Houston: The Centre for Thomistic Studies, 1984); J. Burnell, "The Status of Politics in St. Augustine's City of

hide in caves and monasteries, and if married, homeschool their children; whereas Thomists believe that an engagement with the world is not only virtuous but, some would say, a basal human good.

God," *History of Political Thought* 13, no. 1 (1992): 13–29; Richard A. Crofts, "The Common Good in the Political Theory of Thomas Aquinas," *The Thomist* 37, no. 1 (1973): 155–73; H. A. Deane, *The Political and Social Ideas of St. Augustine* (New York: Columbia University Press, 1963); Robert Dodaro, "Eloquent Lies, Just Wars and the Politics of Persuasion: Reading Augustine's *City of God* in a Postmodern World," *Augustinian Studies* 25 (1994): 77–138; Dodaro, *Christ and the Just Society in the Thought of St. Augustine* (Cambridge: Cambridge University Press, 2004); I. Th. Eschmann, "A Thomistic Glossary on the Principle of the Preeminence of a Common Good," *Medieval Studies* 5, no. 1 (1943): 123–67; Eschmann, "In Defense of Jacques Maritain," *The Modern Schoolman* 22, no. 4 (1945): 183–208; Eschmann, "Studies on the Notion of Society in St. Thomas Aquinas," *Medieval Studies* 8, no. 1 (1946): 1–42; Eschmann, "The Quotations of Aristotle's Politics in St. Thomas *Lectura Super Matthaeum*," *Medieval Studies* 18 (1956): 232–40; J. N. Figgis, *The Political Aspects of St. Augustine's City of God* (Gloucester, MA: Peter Smith, 1963); John Finnis, *Aquinas: Moral, Political and Legal Theory* (Oxford: Oxford University Press, 1998); L. P. Fitzgerald, "St. Thomas Aquinas and the Two Powers," *Angelicum* 56 (1979): 515–56; Ernest Fortin, *Political Realism and Christianity in the Thought of St. Augustine*, The Saint Augustine Lecture Series of Villanova University, 1971 (Philadelphia, PA: Villanova University Press, 1972); Fortin, *Classical Christianity and the Political Order: Reflections on the Theological-Political Problem: Collected Essays*, vol. 2, ed. B. Benestad (London: Rowman and Littlefield, 1996); George J. Lavere, "The Problem of the Common Good in Saint Augustine's *Civitas Terrena*," *Augustinian Studies* 14 (1983): 1–10; C. Harrison, *Augustine: Christian Truth and Fractured Humanity* (Oxford: Oxford University Press, 2000); Charles de Koninck, "In Defence of Saint Thomas: A Reply to Father Eschmann's Attack on the Primacy of the Common Good," *Laval Journal Théologique et Philosophique* 1, no. 2 (1945): 9–109; Charles de Koninck, *Mélanges à la mémoire de Charles de Koninck* (Québec City: Les Presses de l'Université Laval, 1968); J. D. Mac-Queen, "The Origin and Dynamics of Society and the State According to St. Augustine," *Augustinian Studies* 4 (1973): 73–101; Jacques Maritain, *The Person and the Common Good*, trans. John Fitzgerald (Notre Dame, IN: University of Notre Dame Press, 1985); Robert A. Markus, "Two Conceptions of Political Authority: Augustine, *De Civitate Dei* XIX, 14–15 and Some Thirteenth Century Interpretations," *The Journal of Theological Studies* 16 (1965): 68–100; Markus, *Saeculum: History and Society in the Theology of St. Augustine* (Cambridge: Cambridge University Press, 1970); Rex Martin, "The Two Cities in Augustine's Political Thought," *Journal of the History of Ideas* 33, no. 2 (1972): 195–217; *Grace, Politics and Desire: Essays on Augustine*, ed. H. Meynell (Calgary: University of Calgary Press, 1990); John Milbank, *Theology and Social Theory: Beyond Secular Reason* (Oxford: Wiley-Blackwell, 1993); J. Van Oort, *Jerusalem and Babylon: A Study into Augustine's City of God and the Sources of His Doctrine of the Two Cities* (Leiden: Brill, 1991); M. Ruokanen, *Theology of Social Life in Augustine's De civitate Dei* (Göttingen: Vandenhoeck & Ruprecht, 1993); J. V. Schall, *The Politics of Heaven and Hell: Christian Themes from Classical, Medieval and Modern Philosophy* (Lan-

The typical neo-Thomist or Suárezian reading of the reputed differences between Augustine and Aquinas in their approach to the world has been well summarized in the following passage by the late Ernest Fortin of Boston College:

> Aquinas bestowed a degree of autonomy upon the notion of natural law which it never achieved in Augustine's thought. Independently of Revelation and prior to the infusion of divine grace, man has access to the most general principles of moral action and, to the extent to which his will has not been corrupted by sin, finds within himself the power to act in accordance with them. There is thus constituted a specifically natural order apart from, though obviously not in opposition to, the higher order to which human nature is elevated by grace. For the single whole in the light of which man's final end had been discussed by Augustine, two complete and hierarchically structured wholes have been substituted, of which the lower or natural whole possesses its own intrinsic perfection and is capable of operations that do not of themselves require the aid of divine or properly supernatural grace. The issue was not without far reaching practical implications. Speaking figuratively, Augustine had warned that one cannot safely appropriate the spoils of the Egyptians, that is to say, pagan learning and philosophy, without first observing the Passover. Without much exaggeration, one could say that Thomas shows a greater willingness to postpone the celebration of the Passover until the Egyptians have been properly despoiled and, indeed, until such time as the whole land of Canaan has been annexed.[4]

ham, MD: University Press of America, 1984); Y. Simon, "On the Common Good," *The Review of Politics* 6 (October 1944): 530–33; F. Vosman, "Thomas Aquinas, Founder of Modern Political and Social Thought? Aquinas' Political-Ethical Philosophy according to John Finnis," in *Aquinas as Authority*, ed. Paul van Geest, et al. (Leuven: Peeters, 2002); Paul J. Weithman, "Augustine and Aquinas on Original Sin and the Function of Political Authority," *Journal of the History of Philosophy* 30, no. 3 (1992): 353–76; Weithman, "Toward an Augustinian Liberalism," in *The Augustinian Tradition*, ed. G. B. Matthews (Berkeley: University of California Press, 1999); Weithman, "Augustine's Political Philosophy," in *The Cambridge Companion to Augustine*, ed. Eleonore Stump and Norman Kretzmann (Cambridge: Cambridge University Press, 2001).

[4]   Fortin, *Classical Christianity and the Political Order*, 210.

Leaving aside the issue of whether the Suárezian two-tiered theory accurately represents the classical Thomist position, an alternative interpretation is that Augustine and Aquinas were both inclined to annex all fertile parts of the land of Canaan. The classically educated Augustine was not shy about appropriating the spoils of the Egyptians, but both Augustine and Aquinas saw the whole of human history from the perspective of salvation history, in which the achievements of the Hebrews, the Greeks, the Egyptians, and all peoples find their fulfilment, their completion, only in the arrival of Christian Revelation. This is not without significance for interpretations of *Gaudium et Spes* and the Church's engagement with the world.[5] In his endorsement of the Second Vatican Council's pastoral constitution in the 1960s, Jacques Maritain prescribed the document's openness to contemporary intellectual and social currents as the antidote to a neo-Manichean spirit in the preconciliar Church according to which the Church was all good and the world outside her institutions was all bad. Whatever the reasons for the prevalence of such a spirit, it may be argued that it has little to do with approaches to the world to be found in the schools of thought following Augustine or Aquinas. Indeed, it may well be that they are better explained by heretical distortions of the Augustinian and Thomist traditions, such as found, for example, in ecclesial cultures infected with Jansenism and a legalistic ultramontanism.

In his *Commentary on St. John's Gospel*, Aquinas clearly differentiates between three separate meanings for the term "the world" in Sacred Scripture: the creation of God, the creation perfected by Christ, and the perversion of the order of Creation. It is only in the third sense that the world is, as St. John said, "seated in wickedness" (1 John 5:19). Similarly, throughout his works, Augustine distinguishes between the intrinsic goodness of creation and the evil introduced into the world by sin. In *De vera religione* 23.44, he holds that, when Scripture speaks of the world as defiled by human sin, "the world" refers to sinful men, not the material universe. When the material world revolts against the domination of man, the postlapsarian change is in man, not the earth. In his article "St.

---

[5] For an essay on the spoils of the Egyptians theme, including its place in the thought of Augustine, see Étienne Gilson, "Egypte ou Grèce?" *Medieval Studies* 8 (1946): 43–53. For Augustine on the topic, see *De doctrina christiana* 2. See also R. Holte, "*Logos Spermatikos*: Christianity and Ancient Philosophy According to St. Justin's Apologies," *Studia Theologica* 12 (1958), in which Holte observes that Augustine's conclusion was that the classical philosophers had correctly determined the goal, that the skeptics had correctly diagnosed man's inability to attain the goal, and that the goal can be reached only by Christ.

Augustine and Cosmic Redemption," Thomas E. Clarke, S.J., concludes that far from holding onto Manichean attitudes, Augustine was firmly of the view that the "material world lies under no curse, is afflicted with no stain, no subjection to Satan . . . it awaits no redemption, no judgment, no purification. There is no servitude to be broken, no fault to be punished, no stain to be effaced."[6] Nonetheless, both the world in general and man in particular now lie within the dimension of time. They are subject to the forces of death and decay and the reconquest of eternity by man in Christ is an arduous, gradual, and structured process:

> First of all, Christ himself passes through and out of time into eternity, as the model for the Christian pilgrimage. Then it is the turn of man. With faith and baptism the likeness of entity is restored to his higher nature, his "*spiritus*," and is increased in proportion as man turns from "*vanitas*" to "*veritas*." Once more the "*spiritus*" is capable of ruling the "*anima*" and through it the "*corpus*" is thereby rendered purer and freer to give itself to God. And so the peak of man's personality becomes a living sacrifice to God, "*primitiae spiritus*" as divine truth takes hold of this part of man first.[7]

But, while this structural change, indeed divinization, is possible for individuals who cooperate with the work of grace, there is no promise of a forward movement for social life whereby the social order becomes, as Hegel would have it, progressively more rational. History is directional for Augustine only insofar as it is a process of prophecy and fulfilment—it is neither cyclic nor progressive. Nonetheless, as Clarke concludes, the space in which history happens is in no sense an empty space, but rather one that is shaped and structured and completely conditioned by certain categories; since the space belongs to Christ, the Alpha and Omega of all creation or, as John Paul II put it in the first sentence of *Redemptor Hominis*, to "the Redeemer of Man and the Centre and Purpose of Human History."[8] There is thus no theological foundation for a belief that human reason can bring about the perfection of the social order. This was the project of the eighteenth-century philosophers, the nineteenth-century aristocratic

---

[6] Thomas E. Clarke, "St. Augustine and Cosmic Redemption," *Theological Studies* 19 (1958): 133–64, at 150.

[7] Ibid., 157.

[8] Hans Urs von Balthasar, *A Theology of History* (San Francisco: Ignatius Press, 1994), 71.

liberals, and the twentieth-century social engineers. Nonetheless, the argument is often made that just as St. Thomas was prepared to plunder the spoils of the Greeks in the thirteenth century, so also contemporary Thomists should adopt and baptize elements of the Enlightenment traditions construed as having brought about a desirable form of social progress hitherto unachievable by the resources of Christianity alone.

In the context of contemporary Catholic political theology, the question becomes whether the modern nation-state and liberal democracy are logical developments of the classical–theistic syntheses of Augustine and Aquinas or whether they are more accurately understood as heretical reconstructions of these systems. The different responses to this question give rise to two different schools of thought within the Thomist tradition about the engagement of the Church with the world. Those who wish to baptize liberal democracy tend toward the view that its values and principles are in an analogous position to the treasures of the pagan world. However, the position taken by the more "Augustinian Thomists" is that philosophies claiming to be neutral in their stance toward Revelation are not in the same position as pre-Christian systems of thought. Whereas pre-Christian systems were not culpably ignorant, post-Christian systems carry within them, to varying degrees, a rejection of the Holy Spirit's work in convincing the world concerning sin, righteousness, and judgment.[9] While it is often assumed that the situation of the contemporary liberal is analogous to that of the noble pagan, a kind of Marcus Aurelius whose encounter with evil and/or science has left him benignly agnostic, the Oxford Augustinian scholar Oliver O'Donovan has suggested another reading. He argues that the possibilities open to contemporary societies and peoples with a history and memory of the Gospel proclamation do not include naïve malevolence, but only a formation that is demonic to the extent that it is not redeemed and redemptive. For O'Donovan, "the redemptive reality within history becomes the occasion for a disclosure of the historical possibilities of evil, an evil shaped in imitation and replication of the redemptive good."[10]

In Augustinian terms, another way to put the question is to ask whether there is any possibility of the existence of a third, neutral city between the claims of the City of God and the City of Man? Some Au-

---

[9] See John 16: 8–11 and, for a general discussion of this topic, John Paul II, *Dominum et Vivificantem, Acta Apostolica Sedes* 78 (1986).

[10] Oliver O'Donovan, *The Desire of the Nations: Rediscovering the Roots of Political Theology* (Cambridge: Cambridge University Press, 1996), 251.

gustinian scholars, notably Robert Markus, argue for this position, and some authority for it can be found in book 19 of *De civitate Dei*.[11] In this chapter, Augustine acknowledges that the members of both the City of God and the City of Man have a mutual interest in the preservation of a peaceful social order, since "the mortal condition is common to both cities." Members of the City of God are sustained by the goods that belong to the temporal life, "so as more easily to bear the burdens of the corruptible body which presses down on the soul," but unlike members of the City of Man, they are not prone to allowing these things to increase their burdens. The goods of the temporal order "do not deflect them from their progress toward God." They live on earth as pilgrims cooperating with others in "an ordered concord of civic obedience" for the common attainment of things which belong to the mortal life. In a summary paragraph, Augustine concludes:

> For whatever differences there are among the various nations, these all tend towards the same end of earthly peace. Thus, she preserves and follows them, provided only that they do not impede the religion by which we are taught that the one supreme and true God is to be worshipped. And so even the Heavenly City makes use of earthly peace during her pilgrimage, and desires and maintains the co-operation of men's wills in maintaining those things which belong to the mortal nature of man, insofar as this may be allowed without prejudice to true godliness and religion. Indeed, she directs that earthly peace towards heavenly peace.[12]

However, the judgment that Christians and non-Christians may to some degree cooperate in the achievement of temporal goods does not necessarily mean, as Markus suggests, that Augustine points towards a neutral secular space for the state. A raft of contemporary scholars, including O'Donovan, John Milbank, and William T. Cavanaugh, have traced the mutation in the concept of the secular realm from an original sense of simply pertaining to the things of this temporal world to a new sense pertaining to a sphere impervious to the sacred, outside the realm of the theological, where the intrusion of such views is disallowed. They further ar-

---

[11] Markus, *Saeculum*.

[12] St. Augustine, *The City of God* 19, in *International Relations in Political Thought: Texts from the Ancient Greeks,* eds. Chris Brown, Terry Nardin, and Nicholas Rengger (Cambridge: Cambridge University Press, 2002), 134.

gue that within the traditional meaning of the term *saeculum*, society as a whole could never be secular. Rather, "the appearance of a social secularity could only be created by understanding society as a quasi-mechanical system, incapable of moral and spiritual acts," and thus, "the false consciousness of the would-be contemporary secular society lies in its determination to conceal the religious judgments that it has made."[13] Accordingly, Cavanaugh holds that the theory of the neutrality of the contemporary liberal state is itself a kind of *mythos* by which our participation in one another through our creation in the image of God is replaced by the recognition of the other as the bearer of individual rights, which may or may not be given by God, and which serve only to separate what is mine from what is thine.[14] Milbank goes so far as to describe the liberal state as a "virtual circus designed to entertain the middle classes of the privileged world" and the liberal court as a "fiction" whose "dark secret is constitution by a voluntarist theology securing order through the formal regulation of chaos from a single sovereign centre," while Alasdair MacIntyre has described the liberal polity as a site of civil war between the proponents of three rival moral traditions (of which Thomism, very broadly construed to include its patristic antecedents, is but one tradition) held together by the glue of ideological concepts designed to paper over the differences between the contending traditions.[15]

Against the idea that the political realm is, or can be, a theologically neutral territory, Rowan Williams suggests that those who read the *City of God* arrive at the paradox that the only reliable political leader who can be guaranteed to safeguard such authentically political values as order, equity, and the nurture of souls in these things is the man who is, at the end of the day, indifferent to their survival in the relative shapes of the existing order because he knows them to be safeguarded at the level of God's eternal and immutable providence, vindicated in the eternal *civitas Dei*.[16] Williams counsels that this is not to say that Augustine believed that only the saint should be "allowed" to govern, but he did recognize a link between the peace of the temporal order and the virtue of those who live within it and

---

[13] O'Donovan, *The Desire of the Nations*, 247.

[14] W. T. Cavanaugh, *Theopolitical Imagination* (Edinburgh: T & T Clark, 2002), 44.

[15] John Milbank, *Being Reconciled: Ontology and Pardon* (London: Routledge, 2003), 5; Alasdair MacIntyre, *Three Rival Versions of Moral Enquiry: Encyclopedia, Genealogy, and Tradition* (London: Duckworth, 1990); MacIntyre, "Social Structures and their Threats to Moral Agency," *Philosophy* 74 (1999): 311–29.

[16] Rowan Williams, "Politics and the Soul: A Reading of the City of God," *Milltown Studies* 55 (1987): 67.

who are charged with its governance. Gerald Bonner reached the same conclusion, arguing that everything in Augustine's career would suggest that he considered a state governed by Christians to be a better polity than a pagan state, while Robert Dodaro goes even further to suggest that by reading the responses Augustine gives to Christians holding high office, such as found in his *Letter to Macedonius*, one can construct an Augustinian account of political virtue that is linked to the theological virtues.[17] Thus, to acknowledge that Christians and non-Christians have similar temporal needs such as food, clothing, shelter, and peace is not to argue that virtue is irrelevant to the achievement of such goods, or conversely, that the site of this achievement is theologically neutral territory.

Moreover, Augustine's defense of the punishment of heretics remains an anomaly in the theological neutrality theorists are trying to demonstrate. Not only does Augustine countenance the punishment of heresy by civil authorities in *City of God* 19.17, he also makes it clear that there are limits to the civic obedience of Christians, since "it is not possible for the Heavenly City to have laws of religion in common with the earthly city." This means that it will be necessary for Christians to "dissent from the earthly city in this regard, and to become a burden to those who think differently." Indeed, he expects that Christians will have to "bear the brunt of the anger and hatred and persecutions of their adversaries, except insofar as the minds of their adversaries have sometimes been struck by the multitude of the Christians and by the divine aid always extended to them," which is tantamount to saying that, unless a given political order is heavily influenced by Christians and Christian values, Christians should anticipate some degree of persecution. Arguably, this was not a psychological predisposition to pessimism but a realistic appraisal consistent with Christ's teaching in the Gospel of St. John 15:17–21—if they have persecuted me, they will also persecute you. O'Donovan concludes that, "if the Christian community has as its eternal goal, the goal of its pilgrimage, the disclosure of the Church as city, it has as its intermediate goal, the goal of its mission, the discovery of the city's secret destiny through the prism of the Church."[18]

There is nothing therefore in these passages to suggest that the Christian attitude toward the affairs of the world should be one of stoic withdrawal, civic indifference, or theological neutrality. In *De regimine*

---

[17] Gerald Bonner, *God's Decree and Man's Destiny: Studies on the Thought of Augustine of Hippo* (London: Variorum Reprints, 1987).

[18] O'Donovan, *The Desire of the Nations*, 286.

principium, St. Thomas quoted with approval the statement of the pagan Valerius Maximus that, even in matters relating to the dignity of the highest majesty, the city has always affirmed that all things should be placed after religion. And in the same work, he described the duty of a king as one of securing the good life for the community in such a way as to ensure that it is led to the blessedness of heaven. In defining the good life, he quoted from St. Augustine's *De libero arbitrio* 2.19 to the effect that the first and chief requirement of the good life is activity according to virtue, while a sufficiency of bodily goods is an instrumental and secondary requirement. As the Thomist scholar Fr. I. Th. Eschmann noted, "however independent Church and State are, [in the thought of St. Thomas] they do not escape being parts of one *res publica hominum sub Deo, principe universitatis.*"[19]

In the Thomist tradition, the analogue for the idea of a theologically neutral secular space or "third city" is the project of discovering common ground between Liberals and Thomists on the plane of natural law. This is hotly disputed territory, and it is precisely here that the rival interpretations of the relationship between nature and grace have their greatest impact. Those who believe that common ground can be found between the two traditions tend to begin from an extrinsicist account of the relationship between nature and grace, a position associated with the "two ends" theory of human nature: the idea that man's natural end is somehow capable of being distinguished and separated from his supernatural end. Such a position is held explicitly by Germain Grisez of the New Natural Law School and at least implicitly by others in the same school. However, the "two ends" theory has been the subject of extensive criticism from scholars associated with the *Communio* journal, those whom Romanus Cessario, O.P., has described as the Christocentric moralists, and by Denis J. M. Bradley in his work *Aquinas on the Twofold Human Good.*[20] Fortin, who was working outside both the *Communio* and New Natural Law circles, concluded that Aquinas was ambiguous on the related question of whether the natural law is fully defensible on rational grounds or whether its claim to universal acceptability is ultimately based on evidence from Revelation. Nonetheless, in his analysis of Aquinas's treatment of the rela-

---

[19] Eschmann, "St. Thomas on the Two Powers," *Medieval Studies* 20 (1958): 177–205, at 180.

[20] Denis J. M. Bradley, *Aquinas on the Twofold Human Good: Reason and Human Happiness in Aquinas's Moral Science* (Washington, DC: Catholic University of America Press, 1997).

tionship between natural law and the Ten Commandments, Fortin argued that while Aquinas distinguished between the first and second set of commandments, since he regarded the first set as requiring the instruction of human reason by faith, he saw the two tables as in fact inseparable, since the second table logically depends upon the first for its reasonableness. In other words, if there is no God and no transcendent order of goodness, truth, and beauty, then why worry about coveting thy neighbor's wife?

Fortin concluded that "what the Thomistic theory essentially requires is not only that the content of the natural law be naturally known to all men but that it be known precisely as belonging to the natural law, that is to say, to a law which is both promulgated and enforced by God as the author of nature and hence indispensably binding on everyone."[21] In a statement that would resonate well with Augustinians, Fortin drew the conclusion that Thomistic "natural law becomes intelligible only within the framework of a providential order in which the words and deeds of individual human beings are known to God and duly rewarded and punished by him."[22] This means that in societies where atheism and/or agnosticism are common, the project of engaging the world by reference to the natural law tradition will be extremely difficult. In his recent work *Faithful Reason*, John Haldane concludes that anyone reviewing the degree of ideological and moral diversity and conflict exhibited today, half a century after Jacques Maritain's attempt in *The Person and the Common Good*, must wonder how feasible is the project of finding common ground between the Thomist and other traditions with reference to natural law.[23]

Nonetheless, to acknowledge, as Fortin and others have done, that, for both St. Thomas and St. Augustine, the natural law was inextricably linked to the eternal law is not to take the position that it is impossible to engage those who are not fully paid up members of the Thomist and Augustinian traditions. What is, however, required is an openness to theism. In a recent article in *The Thomist* on the subject of pagan virtue, Brian Shanley argued that what Aquinas understood by the nature of acquired moral virtue is essentially political virtue, the virtue of man as a social being ordered to the common good, and that Aquinas believed that such virtue

---

[21] Fortin, *Classical Christianity and the Political Order*, 2:213.

[22] Ibid.

[23] John Haldane, *Faithful Reason: Essays Catholic and Philosophical* (London: Routledge, 2004), 150.

had been not only articulated by the pagans but also actually achieved.[24] However, Shanley suggests that the kind of achievement embodied in the life of pagan political virtue should not be understood as a moral order independent of grace, but rather as the preparation for grace that is already under the influence of grace. The logic of this position would seem to be that we must acknowledge that, while some persons may be "on the side of the angels" or "batting for the City of God," they may not be conscious of doing so. They may be persons of goodwill in need of catechesis. The important Augustinian qualification is "persons of good will." The key Augustinian claim is that, while it may not be exactly clear who is fighting for which team on this side of the final judgment, we are all ultimately (at the final judgment) revealed to be citizens of only one of the two cities, with our membership determined by the objects of our love. This point is well made by Michael Hanby in his work *Augustine and Modernity*.

Against Kant and other proponents of the idea of rationality divorced from love or desire or tradition or revelation, Hanby argues that in making desire intrinsic to all intelligibility Augustine in effect makes doxology the form of all human activity:[25] "This doxologizing of human activity reiterates Augustine's view that all are members incorporate in the bodies of either of the two Adams, citizens of either of the two cities characterized by their respective objects of worship and subject to either of the two mediators. . . . The choice is not 'whether mediation' but between the mediator of life and the mediator of death."[26]

For Hanby, the issue is the Trinity itself and specifically whether or not nature, the meaning of being human, and human agency are understood to occur within Christ's mediation of the love and delight shared as *donum* between the Father and the Son. This is because "it is Christ who determines for Augustine what it means to be human, the Trinity who determines what it means to be and Christ working inseparably with the other Trinitarian personae who incorporates us fully and finally into our being."[27]

The problem with Pelagianism, which Augustine was fighting in his work on the Trinity and to which Ratzinger referred in his criticism of some of the language of *Gaudium et Spes*, is that it institutes a rupture in this Christological and Trinitarian economy, creating possibilities for hu-

---

[24] Brian Shanley, "Aquinas on Pagan Virtue," *The Thomist* 63 (1999): 553–57.

[25] Michael Hanby, *Augustine and Modernity* (London: Routledge, 2003), 64–65.

[26] Ibid., 67.

[27] Ibid.

man nature "outside" the Trinity and the mediation of Christ.[28] From the point of view of salvation history, this is problematic. To quote Cardinal Angelo Scola's gloss on Acts 4:12:

> No other answer, no other foundation will be given to man than the one that has already been laid; but nevertheless man's freedom can fail to ratify the answer that has come to him or her by grace. This framework constitutes the scenario within which history unfolds and to the degree that human freedom withdraws itself from this encounter, the encounter takes on the characteristics of a clash. Man's historical life occurs thus in the sign of the dialectic between the claim of Christ and the *claim of the world*. . . . The claim of Christ is total and it admits no exceptions.[29]

This dialectic between Christ and the world is mediated by the Church, which is not an entity distinct from the world but the world reconciled unto itself and unto God—*mundus reconciliatus ecclesia*—as Fortin noted.[30] While the Church may not be responsible for the governance and administration of the city (outside the Vatican State itself), it cannot be the case that it has no role at all to play in the affairs of the city. There is a marked difference between liberal democracy, on the one hand, and Christian democracy and/or Christian constitutional monarchy, on the other. As Milbank argues, "unlike liberal democracy, Christian democracy has a hierarchic dimension: the transmission of the gift of truth across time, and the reservation of a non-democratic educative sphere concerned with finding the truth, not ascertaining majority opinion."[31]

Those who wish to promote the idea of a theologically neutral third city most commonly rely on the authority of *Gaudium et Spes* §36, which refers to the "autonomy of earthly affairs": "If by the autonomy of earthly affairs we mean that created things and societies themselves enjoy their own laws and values which must gradually be deciphered, put to use, and regulated by men, then it is entirely right to demand that autonomy. Such

---

[28] Ibid., 73.

[29] Cardinal Angelo Scola, "'Claim' of Christ, 'Claim' of the World: On the Trinitarian Encyclicals of John Paul II," *Communio* 18 (Fall 1991): 322–31.

[30] Taken from Augustine's *Sermon* 96, cited in Fortin, *Political Realism and Christianity in the Thought of St. Augustine*, The Saint Augustine Lecture Series of Villanova University, 1971 (Philadelphia, PA: Villanova University Press, 1972), 25.

[31] John Milbank, "The Gift of Ruling: Secularisation and Political Authority," *New Blackfriars* 85 (March 2004): 231.

is not merely required by modern men, but harmonizes also with the will of the Creator. For by the very circumstance of their having been created, all things are endowed with their own stability, truth, goodness, proper laws and order."

This passage is often interpreted as placing limitations on the Church's mediating role between Christ and the world. It is commonly taken to mean that there is no relationship between theology and politics, economics, or the other social sciences. For example, Cardinal Walter Kasper has said that *Gaudium et Spes* was the "Church's recognition of the autonomy of secular fields of activity," that the Council had accepted the "fundamental concept of the modern age," and that "secular matters are to be decided in a secular fashion, political matters in a political fashion, economic matters in an economic fashion."[32] Paradoxically, without further qualifications, such a reading requires a kind of extreme severance of the Church from the world, even though the document is regarded as a general call to Catholics to be more engaged in the life of the world. And it would seem to be inconsistent with the Thomistic understanding of the hierarchical arrangement of goodness in the universe such that individual goods are ordered toward their good in God. An alternative, nonsecularizing reading of this section, proposed by David Schindler, relates it to the analogy of being based on the descent of the Son of God into the world in such a way that worldly realities find their true meaning, precisely as worldly—or indeed "natural"—in their character simultaneously and intrinsically as epiphanies of God's glory.[33] In the *Summa Theologiae* I, q. 85, St. Thomas not only mentions this notion of all things being endowed with their own stability, goodness, and order but also explicitly makes mention of the fact that there are "varying degrees of proportion, species and order corresponding to varying degrees of good." Thus:

> One good is intrinsic to the very substance of human nature, having its own proportion, species and order; this can be neither taken away nor lessened through sin. Another good having its own proportion, species and order is that of the natural inclination to virtue; this can be lessened through sin but not entirely taken away. Again, there is the good of virtue and grace, having its own proportion, species and order; this is wholly destroyed by mortal

---

[32] Walter Kasper, *Faith and the Future* (London: Burns and Oates, 1985), 4.

[33] David Schindler, "Trinity, Creation and the Order of Intelligence in the Modern Academy," *Communio* 28 (Fall 2001): 407.

sin. Finally there is the good which is the rightly ordered human act itself, with therefore its own proportion, species and order; the lack of this good is essentially sin itself.[34]

And similar passages can be found in Augustine's *De Trinitate* 6.12:

> Therefore all these things which are made by divine skill, show in themselves a certain unity, and form, and order; for each of them is both some one thing, as are the several natures of bodies and dispositions of souls; and is fashioned in some form, as are the figures or qualities of bodies, and the various learning and skill of souls; and seeks or preserves a certain order, as are the several weights or combinations of bodies and the loves or delights of souls. When therefore we regard the creator, who is understood by the things that are made we must needs understand the Trinity of whom there appear traces in the creature, as is fitting.[35]

What these passages by Augustine and Aquinas emphasize is the notion of an analogy of being and of a related hierarchy of goodness. One consequence of this is that human persons after the Fall, though intrinsically good, exhibit different degrees of perfection. Thus, in his treatment of the *Imago Dei* in the *Summa Theologiae* I, q. 93, Aquinas distinguished three different ways in which the human person images his creator: first, inasmuch as man possesses a natural aptitude for understanding and loving God; second, inasmuch as man actually or habitually knows and loves God, though imperfectly, in the conformity to grace; and third, inasmuch as man knows and loves God perfectly in the likeness of Glory. While the first is found in all men, the second is found only in the just, and the third only in the blessed. Human dignity based on the notion of the *Imago Dei* is thus a multidimensional concept.

In his call for a more Augustinian Catholic Social Theory, Robert P. Kraynak observed that the Bible (both Old and New Testaments) promoted hierarchies because it understood reality in terms of the "image of God," which is a type of reflected glory—a reflection of something more

---

34 Thomas Aquinas, *Summa Theologiae*, vol. 26, trans. T. C. O'Brien (London: Blackfriars and McGraw-Hill, 1965), 95.

35 *St. Augustine: On the Holy Trinity, Doctrinal Treatises, Moral Treatises,* ed. Philip Schaff, *Nicene and Post-Nicene Fathers, 1st ser., vol. 3* (New York: Cosimo Classics, 2007), 103.

perfect in something less perfect—and that a kind of flattening of the *Imago Dei* to mean simply man's natural aptitude for the exercise of free will and rationality is the decisive factor underlying a dramatic change in Christian politics. This flattened view of the divine image, or vision of the image seen through a Kantian lens, establishes a connection in principle between Christian ethics and a specific political order. For some, Kant has become a father of the Church and working for liberal democracy has become a Christian duty. For Kraynak, the choice is not between Augustine and Aquinas but between Augustine and Kant.

Kraynak further argues that when human rights are joined with democracy, the "subversive thrust of rights and the levelling effects of democracy undermine the hierarchical doctrine of the two cities, undermining the primary claim of the City of God over the earthly city."[36] The gap between the cities becomes closed in such a way that the City of God is difficult to distinguish from the City of man.[37] Moreover, Kraynak claims that the transcendent order loses power in the modern democratic age precisely because it is associated with democracy. When liberal rights are championed by Catholic leaders for institutions beyond the jurisdiction of the Church, it invites the question of why there is a dramatic difference between the structures of the Church and the structures of the world.[38] Can Catholics instilled with the virtues of liberal democracy still concur with Newman that the Church is "not a mere creed or philosophy but a *counter kingdom*" before which all must bow down and lick the dust off her feet so that the world may become a fit object of love?[39]

Against the embrace of the levelling tendencies of the liberal tradition, Kraynak recommends a recovery of St. Augustine's doctrine of the two cities and the proper hierarchies in each order. He observes, however, that the trouble is that contemporary Whig or Kantian Thomists are trying to have it both ways: "In deference to the traditional doctrine of the two cities, they maintain that the Christian message cannot be reduced to

---

[36] Robert P. Kraynak, *Christian Faith and Modern Democracy: God and Politics in a Fallen World* (Notre Dame, IN: University of Notre Dame Press, 2001), 151.

[37] Ibid., 176.

[38] This general orientation toward an emphasis on the rights and preferences of individuals has also had an impact on the Church's liturgical culture. Popular "hymns" such as Deidre Brown's "Come as You Are" and Marty Haugen's "Gather Us In" are decidedly antiperfectionist in orientation.

[39] John Henry Newman, *Sermons Bearing on Subjects of the Day*, first edition, pp. 257 and 120, cited by Christopher Dawson in "St. Augustine and His Age," in *Enquiries into Religion and Culture* (London: Sheed & Ward, 1933), 254.

a particular political order, but they also insist on an intimate connection, even a moral equivalence, between Christianity and liberal democracy based on inalienable human rights."[40]

For Kraynak, the distinction between the two cities means that the spiritual and the political realms are instituted by God and accountable to God but guided by different kinds of law in the service of different ends. The spiritual realm is guided by divine law and an order of charity, holiness, and grace that serves the highest end, eternal salvation. The temporal realm is guided by natural law, which prudence formulates into human or civil law for the secondary ends of the temporal realm. The significance of this distinction, he believes, is that institutions and activities that are prescribed by God for the spiritual realm are governed by divine law, with little flexibility for prudence to adapt them to time and place. Conversely, with regard to the temporal realm, God has not revealed a principle of divine law to determine the major choices and, thus, leaves a huge opening for prudence to operate in politics.[41] For Kraynak, the most important goods of the temporal realm that form the basis of a more authentically Catholic engagement with the world are peace, moral virtue, and civic piety, not the revolutionary trio of equality, liberty, and fraternity. Implicit within this alternative Catholic list of social goods is the recognition of an intrinsic link between virtue, including the theological virtues, and the goods of the temporal realm.

According to this reading, there are elements of the practices of a liberal democratic order that are contrary to the hierarchical and perfectionist spirit of both Augustine and Aquinas. Indeed, Aquinas went so far as to assert that it was not contrary to the dignity of the state of innocence that one person should be ruled by another, since even the angels were ranked into a hierarchy, with one order being called Dominations.[42] Nonetheless, he did distinguish between different understandings of dominion and, in doing so, made reference to Augustine's contrast between dominion and servitude in *De civitate Dei* 19. Clearly any Augustinian or Thomist engagement with the contemporary world will require an analysis of the differing ways in which hierarchies evolve and are legitimated in the rival Augustinian-Thomist, liberal, and post-Nietzschean traditions.

The German theologian Erich Przywara, S.J., developed the notion of theological polarities: for example, the contrast between immanence and

---

[40] Kraynak, *Christian Faith and Modern Democracy*, 182.
[41] Ibid., 184–85.
[42] *ST* I, q. 96, a. 4.

transcendence, between God and the world, and between religion as the ultimate strength of culture and culture as religion's opponent. In the popular perception of the place of the world in the thought of Augustine and Aquinas, there is a polarity, as Przywara might say, between the *contemptus mundi* and the *miseria conditionis humanae*, on the one side, and the *dignitas humanae naturae*, on the other. While Augustine is commonly associated with the first and Aquinas with the second, it would seem that, so long as one reads their work against the backdrop of salvation history, there is no fundamental antagonism between the two traditions in their approach to the world. As Christopher Dawson recognized, in breaking with the tradition of a sacred state, for all his alleged other-worldliness, St. Augustine was the first to make possible the Thomist ideal of a social order resting upon free personality and a common effort towards moral ends.[43]

However, readings of Aquinas that sever the theological Aquinas from the philosophical Aquinas and seek to locate the dignity of human nature in the human capacity for free will or rational intelligence, standing alone without reference to Trinitarian theology and eschatology, will give rise to schools of thought that are fundamentally at odds with Augustinian insights. Conversely, interpretations of Augustine that neglect those elements of his work affirming the Christian engagement with the world will be irreconcilable with the Thomist campaign to annex the whole land of Canaan. Both of these trajectories—on the one hand, the suppression of the Patristic dimension of Aquinas, and on the other, a reading of Augustine as a prisoner of his Manichean heritage—are on the wane in contemporary scholarship, though they continue to be presented as popular caricatures of the two traditions.

In the context of the varied readings of *Gaudium et Spes*, the key Augustinian insights would seem to be that, while the political order is a legitimate theatre for the person in which to work out his or her salvation, one should not expect the New Jerusalem to arrive before the end of time, and one should be very wary of those who claim a passionate concern for justice and the common good from a position of atheism or even agnosticism. The chances are that this concern is but a mask for what Nietzsche recognized as the will to power. Moreover, one should be very wary of closing the gap between the two cities in such a way that the City of God becomes synonymous with liberal democracy. In *The Spirit of the Liturgy*, the Augustinian Ratzinger wrote that "the freedom to give right worship to God, appears, in the encounter with Pharoah, to be the sole purpose of

---

[43] Dawson, "St. Augustine and His Age," 258.

the Exodus, indeed its very essence."[44] In other words, the reason that God liberated the Jews from servitude to the Egyptians was not so that they could enjoy political self-determination as a good in itself, but so that they could order their lives in accordance with God's precept of the priority of worship. Before baptizing any political order, one must at least ask the question, "What place is given to doxology in the rank ordering of the goods of this particular city?"

From a Thomist perspective, the key insights would seem to be that the *Imago Dei* and the notion of human dignity that we take from it are multidimensional concepts. Further, while all things are endowed with their own stability, goodness, and order, there are, nonetheless, "varying degrees of proportion, species and order corresponding to varying degrees of good." There is a need therefore to rehabilitate the concept of hierarchy both in terms of social and political philosophy and in terms of the disciplines themselves such that economic and political questions are not treated as hermetically sealed from the principles of Revelation and salvation history. This is not to argue for a restoration of some particular preliberal social order, but merely to make the point that the liberal tradition is hostile to the notion of hierarchy, unless it is a bureaucratic hierarchy, and that the attempt to baptize liberal democracy places the Thomist tradition in a difficult position of explaining how and where the notion of a hierarchical Church fits within a project that is hostile to models of hierarchy linked to virtue and grace.

The choice therefore is not so much between classical Augustinian theory and classical Thomistic theory, since they both recognized the multidimensional quality of the *Imago Dei* and the impossibility of earthly or social perfection this side of the Second Coming of Christ. The choice is rather between a Catholic social theory conscious of both its Augustinian and Thomist heritage and a Thomism that has jettisoned its Augustinian heritage in favor of Kant. For some, Kant has become a father of the Church. Similarly, the choice is not between reading *Gaudium et Spes* read with Thomist spectacles versus Augustinian spectacles, but between reading the section on the autonomy of earthly affairs with reference to the account of nature and grace in the work of Karl Rahner and reading the same section with reference to the theme of nature and grace in the work of Henri de Lubac. In other words, debates about the interpretation of *Gaudium et Spes* are internal to the Thomist tradition and in general boil down to the conflict between the so-called transcendental Thomism associated

---

[44] Joseph Ratzinger, *The Spirit of the Liturgy* (San Francisco: Ignatius Press, 2000), 20.

with Karl Rahner and the approach to the thought of nature and grace in the works of St. Thomas championed by de Lubac and his *Communio* colleagues. Ratzinger certainly did not side with Rahner's approach, and Wojtyła, while not explicitly rejecting Rahner or explicitly endorsing de Lubac, always argued that *Gaudium et Spes* had to be read through the hermeneutical key of §22. That particular paragraph corresponds, almost word for word, with material in de Lubac's *Catholicism*. Instead of driving a wedge between Wojtyła and Ratzinger or between Thomists and Augustinians, a better approach might be to study more closely the political implications of a choice for Rahner over de Lubac and vice versa.

CHAPTER 4

Variations on the Theme of Christian Hope in the Works of Joseph Ratzinger/ Pope Benedict XVI[1]

THE SIGNIFICANCE OF the Christian theological virtue of hope has been a perennial theme in Pope Benedict XVI's thought from his earliest years as a professor, and motifs that appear in his second encyclical, *Spe Salvi*, were foreshadowed in his earlier academic works.[2] In the shadows behind many of those early works, there stands the influence of Josef Pieper's *Glaube*, *Hoffnung*, and *Liebe*, which were published together in English translation in 1997, and Pieper's *Über das Ende der Zeit*, published in English translation in 1999.[3] Ratzinger himself has acknowledged that

---

[1] First published in *Communio: International Catholic Review* 35, no. 2 (Summer 2008): 200–20.

[2] *Faith and the Future* (Chicago: Franciscan Herald Press, 1971); "Eschatology and Utopia," *Communio* 5 (1978): 211–27; *The Theology of History in St. Bonaventure* (written as an *Habilitationsschrift* in the 1950s and published in English translation in 1971), *Principles of Catholic Theology* (1982); "Vorfragen zu einer Theologie der Erlösung," in *Erlösung und Emanzipation*, ed. L. Scheffczyk (Munich: Herder Verlag, 1982), 167–79; "Gottes Kraft—unsere Hoffnung," *Klerusblatt* 67 (1987): 342–47; "On Hope," *Communio* 12, no. 1 (Spring 1985): 301–15; *Politik und Erlösung* (Opladen: Bachem, 1986); *The Yes of Jesus Christ: Spiritual Exercises in Faith, Hope, and Love* (New York: Crossroad, 1991); and *The End of Time?* (a paper delivered at a meeting of Joseph Cardinal Ratzinger, Johann Baptist Metz, Jürgen Moltmann, and Eveline Goodman-Thau in Ahaus [Mahwah, NJ: Paulist Press, 2004]).

[3] Josef Pieper, *Faith, Hope, Love* (San Francisco: Ignatius Press, 1997), and Pieper, *The End of Time: A Meditation on the Philosophy of History* (San Francisco: Ignatius Press, 1999).

he sought to extend Pieper's philosophical reflections on faith, hope, and love into the theological and spiritual spheres, and his *Spiritual Exercises* were dedicated to Pieper on his eighty-fifth birthday. Behind Pieper, there stands the works of Paschasius Radbertus (ca. 790–865), a Frankish theologian of the Carolingian era, as well as critiques of despair and presumption and the spiritual malady of *acedia* in the moral theology of Augustine and Aquinas. To these Ratzinger adds reflections on hope from St. Bonaventure's *Advent Sermons* and insights from more contemporary, predominately Marxist, authors, such as Ernst Bloch (1885–1977), Max Horkheimer (1895–1973), and Theodore Adorno (1903–1969) of the Institut für Sozialforschung, known colloquially as the Frankfurt School. The significance of these non-Christian authors is that they provide insights into post-Christian analogues for the theological virtue of hope.

In many of the reflections of the Bavarian cardinal/Pontiff, the accent is on how the theological virtue has undergone a secularist mutation. Whereas other scholars have tended to examine the cultures of modernity and postmodernity from the perspective of what they have done to the unity of the transcendentals (for example, Hans Urs von Balthasar), to our understanding of the faculties of the soul and the formation of the "self" (Alasdair MacIntyre and Charles Taylor), to configurations of the nature–grace–culture relationship (Louis Dupré), or to conceptions of good government (Eric Voegelin, Leo Strauss, James V. Schall, and Robert P. Kraynak), Benedict has tended to focus his analysis on its treatment of the theological virtues. In §22 of *Spe Salvi* (an encyclical that can be taken as an antidote to the uncritical affirmation of modernity readings of *Gaudium et Spes*), he stated that "a self-critique of modernity is needed in dialogue with Christianity and its concept of hope."

Central to his reading of this topic is the notion that since the time of the French Revolution the Christian understanding of hope has been mutated into liberal, Marxist, and Social Darwinist notions of progress. He partly came to this judgment through reading the three-volume work of Ernst Bloch on *The Principle of Hope*, which he believes exemplifies the mutation. A critique of the notion of progress as a liberal and Marxist neo-gnostic heresy has also been a recurring theme in the works of such decided non-Marxists as James V. Schall and Eric Voegelin. Schall speaks of a "re-location of the supernatural virtue of hope" in the political philosophy of modernity and recalls that Eric Voegelin characterized the logos of modernity as the "immanentization of the eschaton." Schall argues that, as a result of the tremendous effort of modernity to make philosophy "practical," the classical notions of the last things—death, purgatory, heaven, and hell—have not disappeared altogether but have been relocated *within this world* and reappear in new forms.[4] Liberalism and Marxism thereby parody creedal Christianity rather than transcending it. With Voegelin and Schall, Ratzinger concludes that the liberal and the Marxist images of the world share a "strange eschatological consciousness" ultimately shaped by the idea of progress.[5] He describes the liberal faith in continuous progress as "the bourgeois substitute for the lost hope of faith" and the replacement of the concept of truth by the concept of progress as the "neuralgic point of the modern age."[6] He suggests that "Liberalism and the Enlightenment want to talk us into accepting a world without fear: they promise the complete elimination of every kind of fear" through the application of so-called scientific rationality.[7] Similarly, for Marxists, optimism is the theological virtue of a new god, "history," and a new religion. Heaven becomes the Communist Utopia that is achieved by means of the "revolution," which for its part represents a kind of mythical godhead, as it were, a "God the Son" in relation to the "God the Father" of history.[8] Hope thereby becomes "the virtue of an aggressive ontology, the dynamic force of the march towards Utopia."[9]

The academic merit of the Frankfurt School theorists is that notwithstanding their atheism they offer an immanent critique of the failure of the various post-Enlightenment attempts to ground hope in something other than Christian faith. The major work of value here is *Dialectic of Enlightenment*, coauthored by Adorno and Horkheimer. It is one of the classics of twentieth-century social theory. The following is an excerpt from an entry in the *Stanford Encyclopedia of Philosophy* on its central theses:

> Long before "postmodernism" became fashionable, Adorno and Horkheimer wrote one of the most searching critiques of modernity to have emerged among progressive European intellectuals.

---

4   James V. Schall, "The Encyclical on Hope: On the 'De-immanentizing' of the Christian Eschaton," *Ignatius Insight*, December 3, 2007, accessed March 13, 2017, http://www.ignatiusinsight.com/features2007/schall_onspesalvi_dec07.asp. See also Schall, *The Politics of Heaven and Hell: Christian Themes from Classical, Medieval and Modern Political Philosophy* (Lanham, MD: University Press of America, 1984).

5   Joseph Ratzinger, *The End of Time: The Provocation of Talking about God* (New York: Paulist Press, 2004), 14.

6   Joseph Ratzinger, *The Yes of Jesus Christ: Spiritual Exercises in Faith, Hope, and Love*, 41; Ratzinger, *Values in a Time of Upheaval* (San Francisco: Ignatius, 2006), 88.

7   Ratzinger, *The Yes of Jesus Christ*, 84.

8   Ibid., 42.

9   Ibid.

Dialectic of Enlightenment is a product of their wartime exile. . . . Their book opens with a grim assessment of the modern West: "Enlightenment, understood in the widest sense as the advance of thought, has always aimed at liberating human beings from fear and installing them as masters. Yet the wholly enlightened earth radiates under the sign of disaster triumphant." . . . How can this be, the authors ask. How can the progress of modern science and medicine and industry promise to liberate people from ignorance, disease, and brutal, mind-numbing work, yet help create a world where people willingly swallow fascist ideology, knowingly practice deliberate genocide, and energetically develop lethal weapons of mass destruction? Reason, they answer, has become irrational.

In referring to Adorno and Horkheimer in *Spe Salvi*, Benedict is not endorsing all the principles and conclusions of their Institute for Social Research, but he does demonstrate a knowledge of the secular critiques of modernity that converge with the Catholic criticisms at various junctions. He is sympathetic to their argument that the rationality of the so-called Age of Enlightenment has evinced a propensity for violent applications. These conceptual changes are charted by the pope through the works of Immanuel Kant, particularly his notion of a transition from an ecclesiastical faith to a rational faith presented in 1792 and his later 1794 warning about the consequences if even this so-called rational faith were to be found wanting.

In the series of essays published as *Values in a Time of Upheaval*, Ratzinger further traced the transition from mutations in the concept of God in the eighteenth century (from God the Creator to god the mechanic) to a "second Enlightenment" that renders all conceptions of God, and even of Marxist eschatology and epistemology, obsolete. It takes as its criterion of rationality the experience of technological production based on science. This more contemporary conceptual mutation markets itself under the label of a "new world order." Ratzinger observes that proponents of this concept share with Marxism "the evolutionistic idea that the world we encounter is the product of irrational chance" and "cannot bear any ethical directives in itself as the old idea of nature envisaged."[10] The principles of this new order are therefore not derived from considerations of what is according to nature, but rather from the dreams of scientific and entrepreneurial elites who represent a new ruling class and bring with

---

[10] Ratzinger, *Values in a Time of Upheaval*, 156.

them new forms of coercion, and the greatest scope for their operation lies in the fields of biotechnology. Human life becomes a product, and hope is reduced to something like trust in the future promises of genetic manipulation.

Contrary to all conceptions of rationality that seek to isolate themselves from faith and theology, in §23 of *Spe Salvi*, Benedict reiterates his often repeated statement that "reason needs faith if it is to be completely itself: reason and faith need one another in order to fulfil their true nature and mission," while in §26, against the Social Darwinist values of the new managerial and scientific elites, he makes the point that it is not science that redeems the human person, but rather love.

The culture of modernity is thus held together by numerous concepts, values, and institutional practices that are either severed fragments of an older Christian culture or mutated variations on creedal Christian themes, and the mapping of these transformations has been extensively undertaken in the works of Alasdair MacIntyre, Charles Taylor, and Louis Dupré. In his millennium address to the scholars of the Sorbonne, Ratzinger noted that in the conception of early Christianity the notions of nature, man, God, ethos, and religion were inextricably linked to one another and that precisely this bond helped Christianity to see and navigate clearly amid the crisis of the gods and the crisis of ancient rationality. He implied that the links or "intellectual glue" uniting these various notions have, in successive centuries been detached or, as MacIntyre argues, "severed." He believes that a restoration of these links is a necessary component of the work of evangelization and that one of the most important Patristic insights that requires restoration is the notion that "within the ordering of religion to a rational view of reality, the primacy of the Logos and the primacy of love were revealed to be one and the same":

> The Logos was revealed to be not only the mathematical reasoning at the basis of all things, but as creative love to the point of becoming com-passion, co-suffering with creation. The cosmic aspect of religion which worships the Creator in his power of existence and its existential dimension, the question of Redemption, have co-penetrated one another and become one. . . . [The] evolutionary ethos [of the second Enlightenment], however, which by necessity identifies its key concept in the selection model, hence in the struggle to survive, in survival of the fittest, survival grounded in successful adaptation—has little comfort to offer.

Even in those guises whereby various means people endeavor to embellish it, it remains, ultimately, a cruel ethos.[11]

The linking of love and knowledge is a common Augustinian and Balthasarian motif. In *A Theological Anthropology*, a work praised by Ratzinger, Balthasar linked the logos of love and knowledge with the theological virtues in the following manner: "Such unity of the Christian attitude of faith, hope and love is the ultimate basis of Christian understanding or knowledge, whose nearest analogy is the knowledge of a beloved human being. . . . The mediator of such understanding in love is the Holy Spirit which, as the 'Spirit of Childhood,' encourages two attitudes. The first is the immediate, open approach to all the treasures and secrets of God; the second is the childlike spirit which does not presume to take what does not belong to it."[12]

This notion of the need for childlike receptivity to the work of the Holy Spirit steers the Catholic faith away from the tendency to present the faith as an intellectual system requiring mostly sound philosophical foundations for its comprehension. While not dismissing the need for sound philosophy, in his first two encyclicals, Benedict emphasized the more personalist or affective dimensions of the act of comprehension, the response of the human heart to God. In *Spe Salvi*, he adds to this the theme that love transcends time: "the saints' way of acting and living is de facto a 'proof' that the things to come, the promise of Christ, are not only a reality that we await, but a real presence."[13] We believe not only because something is logically coherent but also because we have seen the beliefs embodied in the practices of the lives of the saints, whose love for others is what makes belief plausible and persuasive, even compelling. Here affirmed is the epistemic role of the saints as the most authentic witnesses to the truth about existence to which reference was made by John Paul II in *Fides et Ratio*.

The mission of the saints then links to another significant subtheme of *Spe Salvi*, that salvation is a social mission: "No one lives alone. No one sins alone. No one is saved alone. The lives of others continually spill over into mine: in what I think, say, do and achieve. And conversely, my life spills over into that of others: for better and for worse. . . . Our hope

---

[11] Joseph Ratzinger, Sorbonne Address, "2000 Years after What?" The Sorbonne, Paris, November 27, 1999, quoted from a translation by Maria Klepecka based on the Polish translation published in *Christianitas* 3, no. 4 (2000): 11–23.

[12] Hans Urs von Balthasar, *Theological Anthropology* (New York: Sheed & Ward, 1967), 97.

[13] Pope Benedict XVI, *Spe Salvi*, §8.

is always essentially also hope for others; only thus is it truly hope for me too."[14] In this context, Benedict cites Henri de Lubac's ecclesiological masterpiece *Catholicism: Christ and the Common Destiny of Man* as a place to gain an understanding of this point. In a preface to the 1988 English translation of the work, he described it as "an essential milestone on my theological journey" in which de Lubac demonstrated "how the idea of community and universality, rooted in the Trinitarian concept of God, permeates and shapes all the individual elements of Faith's content."

Part of Ratzinger's concern here is the power of what in other places he has called "pious Pelagianism" and a "narrow-minded individualistic Christianity." He has complained that pious Pelagians think of the Christian life as something like taking out an insurance policy against spending eternity in hell. They want security, not hope:

> By means of a tough and rigorous system of religious practices, by means of prayers and actions, they want to create for themselves a right to blessedness. What they lack is the humility essential to any love—the humility to be able to receive what we are given over and above what we have deserved and achieved. The denial of hope in favour of security that we are faced with here rests on the inability to bear the tension of waiting for what is to come and to abandon oneself to God's goodness. This kind of Pelagianism is thus an apostasy from love and from hope but also at the profoundest level from faith too. . . . The core of Pelagianism is a religion without love that in this way degenerates into a sad and miserable caricature of religion.[15]

Against the mentality of the pious Pelagians, Pope Benedict wants to emphasize that Christian life is a group exercise and that those who are brothers and sisters in Christ can continue to help one another even if they are separated by death. Thus, in §48 of *Spe Salvi* we find the following statement: "The belief that love can reach into the afterlife, that reciprocal giving and receiving is possible, in which our affection for one another continues beyond the limits of death—this has been a fundamental conviction of Christianity throughout the ages and it remains a source of comfort today."

While the pious Pelagians err by focusing on their own salvation and

---

[14] Ibid.
[15] Ratzinger, *The Yes of Jesus Christ*, 82.

turning it into a project to be realized by a strategic plan that, once enacted, should evoke a predictable reward from God, others can err in the opposite direction. They want to believe that there are no eternal consequences of our life choices here and now, that everyone is automatically guaranteed an entry ticket to an egalitarian heaven where it does not matter what one has made of the gift of life on earth. Against this mentality Pope Benedict offers the following words of caution: "Grace does not cancel out justice. It does not make wrong into right. It is not a sponge which wipes everything away, so that whatever someone has done on earth ends up being of equal value. Dostoevsky, for example, was right to protest against this kind of Heaven and this kind of grace in his novel *The Brothers Karamazov*. Evildoers, in the end, do not sit at table at the eternal banquet beside their victims without distinction, as though nothing had happened."[16]

A variation on this kind of presumption of a universal sponging is what Pope Benedict calls "bourgeois Pelagianism." He describes it as symptomatic of the following attitude: "if God really does exist and if he does in fact bother about people he cannot be so fearfully demanding as is described by the faith of the Church. Moreover I'm no worse than the others: I do my duty, and the minor human weaknesses cannot really be as dangerous as all that." [17] Here his use of the adjective "bourgeois" should not be construed to mean literally "middle class," but rather having a preference for that which will get one by, rather than striving for excellence. A number of European sociologists have used the expression in this way, including Werner Sombart, who argued that Protestant cultures tend to be bourgeois, while Catholic cultures tend to be "erotic" and aristocratic. Here "erotic" does not mean "explicitly sexual," but rather passionate, or driven by transcendent ideals. The bourgeois personality type makes do with what is serviceable and is content to just get across the line while the aristocratic personality type always wants the best. The corrosive effect of the bourgeois mentality on Catholic spirituality and the theological virtue of hope was a recurring theme in the novels of the French writer Georges Bernanos, and thus, reading Bernanos helps to place Ratzinger's use of this expression into a richer spiritual context. One example of Bernanos's treatment of this theme, which includes elements of both pious and bourgeois Pelagianism, can be found in the following paragraph taken from *Nous autres Français*:

---

[16] *Spe Salvi*, §44.
[17] Ratzinger, *The Yes of Jesus Christ*, 81.

There exists a Christian order. . . . This order is the order of Christ, and the Catholic tradition has preserved its essential principles. But the temporal realization of this order does not belong to the theologians, the casuists, or the doctors, but to us Christians. And it seems that the majority of Christians are forgetting this elementary truth. They believe that the Kingdom of God will happen all by itself, providing they obey the moral rules (which, in any event, are common to all decent people), abstain from working on Sunday (if, that is, their business doesn't suffer too much for it), attend a Low Mass on this same day, and above all have great respect for clerics. . . . This would be tantamount to saying that, in times of war, an army could quite fulfill the nation's expectations if its men were squeaky clean, if they marched in step behind the band, and saluted their officers correctly.[18]

Often, bourgeois Pelagians react strongly against all criticisms of secularizing post-conciliar practices and the concerns of those who worry that there might be problems with the reception of the conciliar call for renewal and with popular interpretations of conciliar documents. When presented with statistical data about plummeting Mass attendance rates, the even smaller numbers going to Confession, and the rather large numbers cohabiting before marriage, contracepting, and so on, the bourgeois Pelagians are likely to reply that younger post-conciliar generations simply have different ways of expressing their spirituality. Against these kinds of reactions Ratzinger has spoken of the "arrogance of apostasy which is a parody of faith and hope."[19] He has also drawn analogies between the attitudes of contemporary bourgeois Pelagians and those who imprisoned the prophet Jeremiah for his pessimism. He observes that, in the time of Jeremiah "the official optimism of the military, the nobility, the priesthood, and the establishment prophets demanded the conviction that God would protect his city and his temple." However, they were all wrong. They ignored all the evidence to the contrary and "downgraded God to become the guarantee of human success and the justification for their irrationalism."[20] Contrary to the attitude that whatever appears to be wrong with the contemporary Church must somehow be the work of the Holy Spirit,

---

[18] English translation comes from Hans Urs von Balthasar, *Bernanos: An Ecclesial Existence* (San Francisco: Ignatius, 1996), 555.

[19] Ratzinger, *The Yes of Jesus Christ*, 41.

[20] Ibid., 50.

even if it is not obvious how or why, Ratzinger has written that the criterion that Jeremiah laid down remains valid: "the proclamation of empirical success is to be judged by empirical criteria and cannot rely on theology."[21] He also notes that, although Jeremiah came across to his peers as nothing but an annoying pessimist, it was his words composed during the seventy years exile that Christ was ultimately to quote at the Last Supper.

Implicit within the mentality of the bourgeois Pelagians is a form of trust in the liberal notion of progress. Even the cavalier attitude toward the rejection of the Church's moral teachings suggests an acceptance of the view that the changing social attitudes of the 1960s represent progress rather than decline. Ratzinger has consistently rejected all the versions of belief in cumulative progress. With reference to the Revelation of St. John in the New Testament, he remarks that "the vision of history that is displayed there represents the greatest possible antithesis one can imagine to faith in perpetual progress."[22] Even more emphatically, he stated. "The Apocalypse is far removed from the promise of continual progress: still less does it recognize the possibility of establishing a once and for all fortunate and definite form of society through our own human activity. Despite or rather precisely because of this rejection of irrational expectations it is a book of hope."[23]

As Benedict XVI, he reiterated this point, contrary to much of the post-conciliar Whiggish thinking that saw in contemporary Western liberalism a qualitative ethical advancement over previous forms of social organization. Whereas in the late 1940s Jacques Maritain spoke of a "kind of plant life formation and growth of moral knowledge and feeling, in itself independent of philosophic systems and the rational justifications they propound," in §24 of *Spe Salvi*, Benedict offered the following reflections:

> Let us ask once again: what may we hope? And what may we not hope? First of all, we must acknowledge that incremental progress is possible only in the material sphere. Here, amid our growing knowledge of the structure of matter and in the light of ever more advanced inventions, we clearly see continuous progress towards an ever greater mastery of nature. Yet in the field of ethical awareness and moral decision-making, there is no similar possibility of accumulation for the simple reason that man's freedom is always

---

[21] Ibid., 51.
[22] Ibid., 53.
[23] Ibid., 55.

new and he must always make his decisions anew. . . . Naturally, new generations can build on the knowledge and experience of those who went before, and they can draw upon the moral treasury of the whole of humanity. But they can also reject it, because it can never be self-evident in the same way as material inventions. The moral treasury of humanity is not readily at hand like tools that we use; it is present as an appeal to freedom and a possibility for it.

Much of the above can be succinctly summarized in Pieper's statement that "the classical theology of the Church is equally removed from both the over simplification of liberalism and the desperate rigidity of stoicism."[24]

These two Pelagian spiritual pathologies can also be read as particular manifestations of what Augustine and Aquinas identified as the sins of despair and presumption. Ratzinger has noted that the two attitudes are very close to one another and inwardly coincide. The error they share is the idea that one does not need God for the realization and fulfilment of one's own being.[25] Thus, "those who despair do not pray anymore because they no longer hope: those who are sure of themselves and their own power do not pray because they rely only on themselves."[26] Despair and depression, common conditions in the contemporary Western world, are directly linked by Ratzinger to secularism. Those who have no relationship with Christ are bound to experience a certain emptiness and hopelessness. A secularist culture impoverishes spiritual horizons and diminishes opportunities for self-transcendence. Even Ratzinger's well known aversion to rock music is rooted in his judgment that its popularity can be explained by its pseudoliturgical character. It is a kind of pathetic attempt by entrepreneurial elites to make money out of the human need for an experience of ritual and self-transcendence. The evangelization of youth thus requires their liberation from the horizons of mass culture and an encounter with Christ that is authentically sacramental. Ratzinger paternally diagnoses their condition with specific reference to the theological virtues: "Thus today we often see in the faces of young people a remarkable bitterness, a resignation that is far removed from the enthusiasm of youthful adventures into the unknown. The deepest root of this sorrow is the lack of any great hope and the unattainability of any great love: everything one can

---

[24] Josef Pieper, *Faith, Hope, Love* (San Francisco: Ignatius Press, 1997), 130.

[25] Ratzinger, *The Yes of Jesus Christ*, 81.

[26] Ibid., 67.

hope for is known, and all love becomes the disappointment of finiteness in a world whose monstrous surrogates are only a pitiful disguise for profound despair."[27]

Although Ratzinger is often portrayed as an Augustinian, which is certainly an accurate depiction, it is noteworthy that, in this context, he closely follows Pieper's judgment that *acedia* (a kind of spiritual slothfulness) is a symptom of secularization and the underlying Thomist analysis that it stems from a lack of greatness of soul (*magnanimitas*), from an incapability of believing in the greatness of the human vocation that has been destined for us by God. In his *Spiritual Exercises*, Ratzinger quoted extensively from St. Thomas's treatment of hope and listed each of the "daughters of *acedia*" whose pedigree was tracked by Aquinas:

> Along with despair there is the "footloose restlessness of the mind," for, as Thomas says, "no man can dwell in sorrow." If the foundation of the soul is sorrow we are faced with a continual flight of the soul from itself, with a profound restlessness man is afraid to be alone with himself. He loses his center and becomes a mental and spiritual vagabond who is always out. The symptoms of this footloose restlessness are garrulousness and inquisitiveness. Further there is inward restlessness (*importunitas—inquietudo*) and changeability of will and purpose (*instabilitas loci vel propositi*).[28]

Other "daughters" include: apathy (*torpor*) with regard to the things necessary for salvation, faintheartedness (*pusillanimitas*), nursing grudges (*rancor*), and spitefulness (*militia*).[29]

In various of his works, but particularly in his Christmas reflection on art in the Basilica of Saint Mary Major, Ratzinger linked the theological virtue of hope to the transcendental of beauty and its absence to a rationality severed from all affectivity. He noted that "depression and despair result when the balance of our feelings becomes disordered or even suspended, when we no longer perceive with our hearts, but merely with a knowledge that has lost its roots."[30] This is Ratzinger in a very Augustinian moment.

---

[27] Ibid., 73.

[28] Ibid., 78.

[29] Ibid.

[30] Ratzinger, *Images of Hope: Meditations on Major Feasts* (San Francisco: Ignatius Press, 2006), 22.

In other places he has commended Augustine for his recognition that "the necessary purification of sight takes place through faith (Acts 15:9) and through love, at all events not as a result of reflection alone and not at all by man's own power."[31] In this reflection, he added a criticism of Cartesian rationality, or what Bernanos has called "the logos of the machine": "Some things are discerned, not through domination, but only through service, and these are the higher ways of perception. For what we are able to dominate is beneath us. A thinking that persists in dissecting and putting together is in its essence materialistic and reaches only to a certain threshold. So beyond dissecting and analyzing, the physician needs dedication to the person in whom the characteristics of the sickness appear."[32]

While Christ is the Way, the Truth, and the Life, one path to him is by the contemplation of the beauty of creation, including beauty that has been created by human hands and voices. The transcendental quality of beauty and the theological virtues of faith, hope, and love are intimately connected to our perception of the Truth. This theme was also taken up by Ratzinger in a Christmas reflection on the Basilica of Saint Mary Major. Within the Basilica there stands an arch of triumph above a crypt that was originally built as a replica of the cave of Bethlehem. On this, Ratzinger reflected: "The interaction of arch of triumph and cave teaches us to pass from aesthetics to faith. . . . The transition to this image can lead us a step further still. It helps us to loosen faith from the strain of will and intellect and allow it to enter into the whole of our existence. It gives aesthetics back to us in a new and greater way: if we have followed the call of the Savior, we can also receive anew the language of the earth, which he himself assumed."[33]

This epistemology is of course deeply Trinitarian. The theological virtues and the transcendentals work together in a symphony. Pieper, quoting from St. Thomas's questions on hope, says that the theological virtues flow back upon themselves in a sacred circle: one who is led to love by hope has thereafter a more perfect hope, just as he also believes now more strongly than before. Moreover:

> The existential relationship of these three—faith, hope, and love—can be expressed in three sentences. First: faith, hope, and love have all three been implanted in human nature as natural

---

[31] Ratzinger, "*Gaudium et Spes*," in *Commentary on the Documents of Vatican II*, ed. Herbert Vorgrimler, vol. 3 (New York: Herder and Herder, 1969), 155.

[32] Ratzinger, *Images of Hope*, 39–40.

[33] Ibid., 21–22.

inclinations (*habitus*) conjointly with the reality of grace, the one source of supernatural life. Second: in the orderly sequence of the active development of these supernatural inclinations, faith takes precedence over both hope and love; hope takes precedence over love; conversely, in the culpable disorder of their dissolution, love is lost first, then hope, and last of all, faith. Third: in the order of perfection, love holds first place, with faith last, and hope between them.[34]

Similarly, Balthasar observed that St. Paul binds faith, hope, and love together in a sort of *perichoresis*.[35] Just as he traced the severance of the beautiful from the true and the good in the transition from Christendom to the culture of modernity, so too one could trace the severance of each of the theological virtues from their *perichoretic* relationship and their subsequent secularist mutations. In his first two encyclicals, Pope Benedict broke the ground on this genealogy with his reflections on the severance of *eros* from *agape* and the rise of mutant versions of Christian hope.

This issue of the severance of the Trinitarian relationships between faith, hope, and love is, however, only one aspect of a much broader problem identified by Ratzinger in his *Principles of Catholic Theology* as no less than the "fundamental crisis of our age." He summarizes it as "coming to an understanding of the mediation of history within the realm of ontology."[36] In retrospect, this crisis can be seen to be at the center of almost all the theological controversies of the twentieth century, resting as it does on conceptions of the relationships between nature and grace (as one problem) and among nature, grace, and culture (as a further compounded problem). It was central to the modernist controversy at the turn of the century and to the conflicts over nature and grace that arose in the 1940s and still remain unresolved. It is also an essential component of conflicts in the territories of ecclesiology and moral theology, and it lies at the heart of the divisions between Catholics and Protestants. As Ratzinger noted, "many Protestants have sought to reject categories of being and describe faith as salvation in purely historical terms, to solve the problem of history's mediation in the realm of ontology by cancelling it and declaring

---

34 Pieper, *Faith, Hope, Love*, 103.

35 Hans Urs von Balthasar, *A Theology of History* (San Francisco: Ignatius Press, 1994), 44.

36 Joseph Ratzinger, *Principles of Catholic Theology* (San Francisco: Ignatius Press, 1982), 160.

history alone to be that which is and is essential."[37] In *Principles of Catholic Theology*, he further observed that the shocks to historical consciousness produced by two world wars and the arrival of the secular city in the 1960s pushed the problem of salvation history with a new urgency into the center of theological speculation. As a consequence, by the 1980s, Ratzinger was distinguishing between two stages in this theological speculation:

> First ... [the treatment of issues such as] Platonism and Christendom, Hellenization and de-Hellenization, ontology and history, institution and event, incarnational theology and the theology of the cross, ... [which can be summarized as the issue] of the relationship between history and ontology, of the question of the mediation of history in the realm of ontology; secondly a more revolutionary type of questioning, which, through the intermediate stage of the theology of hope, refers history essentially to the future. ... In the form of a theology of revolution or liberation, ... the theme of discontinuity is molded into a new form: where history is salvation only on the basis of hope, past history is rejected as a form of existence; talk of the historically conditioned becomes the antipode of a turning to the historical.[38]

In *Principles of Catholic Theology* Ratzinger did not attend to the task of providing a definitive resolution of the crisis, though he did argue that Karl Rahner's attempt to deal with the issue in *Hearers of the Word* made the mistake of making man's being itself historical in character.[39] In this, he follows Pieper's criticisms of the influence of Heidegger. In his essay "On Hope," Pieper wrote: "Present day existential philosophy, which regards human existence exclusively in its temporality as a 'being in time' is right to the extent that it opposes an idealistic doctrine of man in which the *status viatoris* seems transformed, against its nature, into a permanent likeness to God. But to the extent that this existential philosophy conceives of man's existence as essentially and 'in the foundation of its being temporal' (Heidegger), it too fails to comprehend the true nature of its subject."[40]

---

[37] Ibid., 158.
[38] Ibid., 158–59.
[39] Ibid., 162.
[40] Pieper, *Faith, Hope, Love*, 95.

More fundamentally, Pieper observed that "Existentialism fails to recognize the true nature of human existence because it denies the 'pilgrimage' character of the *status viatoris*, its orientation toward fulfilment beyond time, and hence, in principle, the *status viatoris* itself."[41] While Rahner did not himself deny the *status viatoris*, he tended to conflate salvation history with world history and thereby, unwittingly, downplayed the theo-dramatic element in individual human lives. As Ratzinger expressed the problem:

> Rahner appropriated universal reason for Christianity and tried to prove that universal reason leads ultimately to the teachings of Christianity and that the teachings of Christianity are the universally human, the rational par excellence. In the generation that followed Rahner the direction of his thought was reversed. If the teachings of Christianity are the universally human, the generally held views of man's reason, then it follows that these generally held views are what is Christian. If that is the case, then one must interpret what is Christian in terms of the universal findings of man's reason.[42]

Based on such presumptions, the liberation theologians of the 1970s and 80s sought to develop a theology upon a Marxist epistemology and eschatology. Against Rahner's treatment of the relationship between history and ontology, Ratzinger suggested that "we must comprehend why God's universalism (God wants everyone to be saved) makes use of the particularism of the history of salvation (from Abraham to the Church)," and, further, that "concern for the salvation of others should not lead to this particularism being as good as completely deleted: the history of salvation and the history of the world should not be declared to be simply identical because God's concern must be directed at everyone."[43] Ratzinger further indicated that he thought Balthasar's notion of "seeing the whole in the fragments" was a better approach to the problem. In this context, he made specific reference to Balthasar's 1963 work *Das Ganze im Fragment*, which was published in English in 1967 as *A Theological Anthropology*. Here Balthasar made the following observations with specific reference to the theological virtues:

---

[41] Ibid.

[42] Ratzinger, *Principles of Catholic Theology*, 168.

[43] Ratzinger, *The Yes of Jesus Christ*, 92.

Faith, hope and charity move through a fragmentary existence towards an unforeseeable perfection. Therefore, they can become suspicious if wholeness is offered recognizably and tangibly to them in advance. In the fragmentary nature of man and the world they have a guarantee of the genuine. As a blind man feels with knowing hands the sharp edges of broken pottery, so they learn from the fragments of existence in what direction toward wholeness God points them. Such a fragment is, for groping human hands, the cross of Christ: innumerable lines of significance intersect at it, disentangle, then entangle themselves again. A synthesis that can be grasped at a glance is all the less possible in that the synthesis that God brought about manifested itself in the ultimate shattering of all human plans, demands and longings. Faith, love and hope grope their way through the darkness: they believe the incredible; they love that which withdraws itself, abandoning them; they hope against hope. The darkness with its withdrawal of all available unity makes them one.[44]

Ratzinger's criticism of Rahner also echoes Pieper's earlier criticisms of Teilhard de Chardin. At a conference in Paris in 1951, Pieper was critical of Chardin's theology of history on the grounds that it could not account for the meaning of martyrdom. In Pieper's words, "evolution knows no martyrs."[45] If one is living in a low stage of historical or, in Chardin's language, "cosmic" development, why die for something that might turn out not to be an eternal value or principle after all? In *The End of Time* essay, Ratzinger summarized Chardin's project in the following words: "For Teilhard, the Eucharist appears as the anticipation of the transformation and divinization of matter, as the compass needle orienting the cosmic movement. For Teilhard, all of evolution's terrible aspects and so too, finally, all of history's atrocities, are inevitable mishaps in the process of upward movement toward the definitive synthesis. . . . Thus, in the end human beings in their suffering appear as the material for evolution's experiment, the world's injustices as mishaps that you have to reckon for such a journey. Humanity is subordinated to the cosmic process."[46] Against the logic of this orientation, Ratzinger argues that "the cosmos is not neutral when it comes to human beings. Human beings are not beggarly parasites of being;

---

[44] Von Balthasar, *Theological Anthropology*, 95–96.

[45] Ratzinger, *The End of Time*, 16.

[46] Ibid., 15.

rather, the cosmos is created with freedom in mind, a freedom that takes up its inner trajectories and alone can bring them to their goal."[47]

Nonetheless, while Ratzinger clearly regards human nature as a constant in creation that does not cumulatively develop to some higher ontological stage, either in its capacity for love or for knowledge (at least not before the Last Judgment and the renewal of the cosmos), he also recognizes that the possibilities for participation in the life of the Trinity, for deepening love and knowledge, can be either thwarted or enhanced by cultures that are more or less impervious or receptive to grace and the cultivation of virtue. It is the element of creative freedom within human nature that is so vulnerable to damage from a secularist culture. The severance of the links between notions of God, human nature, ethos, and religion and the emergence of counterfeit notions of faith, hope, and love set limits on the intellectual horizons of people at the same time as encouraging social and institutional practices that require a capacity for vice rather than virtue and thereby diminish a person's ability to love.

In *Spe Salvi*, Pope Benedict draws attention to the similarities between the state of society when the *First Letter to the Corinthians* was written and the state of contemporary Western culture: myth had lost its credibility; the Roman state religion had become fossilized into simple ceremony that was scrupulously carried out, although by then, it was merely a "political religion"; and philosophical rationalism had confined the gods within the realm of unreality. Today, many people no longer even understand what Christian revelation is, let alone have the capacity to make a judgment about its credibility. In some countries, for example, the United Kingdom, the state religion has for the most part been fossilized into simple ceremony, while in other countries, for example, the United States, the pseudo–state religion is provided by nationalism, capitalism, and the liberal tradition, or a blend of all of them and, in most places, it is politicians, rather than priests, who offer redemption, by means of scientific and economic progress. In his speech to the bishops of Mexico delivered in Guadalajara in 1996, Ratzinger concluded that, "when politicians want to bring redemption, they promise too much. When they presume to do God's work, they do not become divine but diabolical." In his *Spiritual Exercises in Faith, Hope, and Love*, he concluded:

A society that turns what is specifically human into something purely private and defines itself in terms of a complete secularity

---

[47] Ibid., 22.

(which moreover inevitably becomes a pseudo-religion and a new all-embracing system that enslaves people)—this kind of society will of its nature be sorrowful, a place of despair: it rests on a diminution of human dignity. A society whose public order is consistently determined by agnosticism is not a society that has become free but a society that has despaired, marked by the sorrow of man who is fleeing from God and in contradiction with himself. A Church that did not have the courage to undermine the public status of its image of man would no longer be the salt of the earth, the light of the world, the city set on a hill.[48]

---

[48] Ratzinger, *The Yes of Jesus Christ*, 77.

CHAPTER 5

Culture in the Thought of John Paul II and Benedict XVI[1]

MY TOPIC IS the concept of culture in the thought of St. John Paul II and Pope Benedict XVI. As a concept, it is to be found in patristic scholarship in the context of issues surrounding the conversion of pagan peoples (and indeed, St. Basil the Great had something to say on the subject), but it slipped from being an issue of theological prominence in the medieval period as Christian civilization became more consolidated and there were fewer pagan peoples in nearby villages to convert. It re-emerged as a theme in the works of German scholars in the late-eighteenth and nineteenth centuries and in the works of sociologists such as Max Weber, Werner Stark, and Werner Sombart in the early twentieth century. Weber, Stark, and Sombart were fascinated by the differences between Catholic and Protestant cultures. Claudio Veliz used Isaiah Berlin's metaphors of the fox and the hedgehog to describe them: British Protestantism is represented by the Gothic fox and Spanish Catholicism by the Baroque hedgehog. There are, of course other Protestant cultures besides the British and other Catholic cultures besides the Spanish, but these two have tended to dominate the literature.

After the French Revolution of 1789, German scholars became absorbed in the question of why the revolution had occurred in France rather than in Germany. They concluded that it had something to do with the strong Roman foundations of French culture and the comparatively stronger influence of the Greeks over the world of German letters. In the schol-

---

[1]   Originally presented as the Archbishop J. Michael Miller Award Lecture at the University of St. Thomas in Houston in 2010.

arship that followed, three separate words were used for what in English is covered by the one word "culture." The Germans spoke of *Kultur*, which would be translated as "civilization" in English; *Bildung*, or "self-development" or "education" in English; and *Geist*, which literally means "spirit" but corresponds to what in English is usually rendered by the Greek word *ethos*. So, *Kultur* refers to culture in its widest sense as a civilization, as in the expression "Western culture" or "Islamic culture." *Bildung* always relates to the education and development of individuals, and *Geist* refers to the cultures of institutions, such as the ethos of a school, hospital, or university.

As a generalization, one might suggest that the pontificate of John Paul II addressed itself to the problems of culture in the sense of *Kultur* and *Geist*, the cultures of civilizations and institutions, whereas Benedict's interventions, both as a cardinal and as pope, focused more on the notion of culture as *Bildung*, on the self-development of individuals. Both pontiffs were concerned that Catholics are living and maturing within cultures—in all three senses of the term—that are hostile to the faith. In biblical language, we might say that the soil in which the seeds of the faith are to grow is barren. This is particularly a problem in the Western world. In other parts of the world, there are different problems. For example, in Asia, Christians often find themselves as minorities in cultures that are predominately Islamic or Buddhist, or in the case of China, Vietnam, and North Korea, cultures that retain some residue of Marxism. While both pontiffs have addressed themselves to the problems of Catholics living within these cultures, this paper will focus on the problems of what was the Christian West.

An intellectual history of how the soil of Western Christendom became barren would take us on a long journey back at least as far as the fourteenth century, and there is not time for that journey here. Instead, we will begin the analysis in 1964. Just prior to his opening of the final session of the Second Vatican Council, Pope Paul VI, in his encyclical *Ecclesiam Suam*, complained of a rising tide of secularism within the Church, and he was critical of those who thought that the "reform of the Church should consist principally in adapting its way of thinking and acting to the customs and temper of the modern secular world." He observed that this "craving for uniformity" is observable even in the realm of philosophy, especially in ethics, and he reiterated the Gospel counsel to be "in the world but not of it." A decade later, in 1975 in his apostolic exhortation *Evangelii Nuntiandi*, he acknowledged that the modern world seems to be "forever immersed in what a modern author [Henri de Lubac] has termed 'the drama of atheistic humanism.'" He concluded that "the split between the Gospel and culture is undoubtedly the tragedy of our time" and "that a faith that does not affect a person's culture is a faith not fully embraced, not entirely thought out, not faithfully lived."

This split between the Gospel and culture becomes, in the papacy of John Paul II, the conflict between "the civilization of love" and the "culture of death." This culture of death is not something that can be defined in the breadth of one sentence. Of course, it has become a polite, short-hand expression for the abortion industry, but at a deeper level, it is connected to certain dispositions toward the meaning of life and love, and it has far ranging consequences that extend beyond beginning and end-of-life issues. It includes a preference for power and self-sufficiency over love and over the danger of personal vulnerability. It is stoic in the sense of giving priority to the head over the heart. It is pragmatic rather than idealistic. It is a disenchanted culture wherein concepts like grace, sacraments, and mystery have no place. It sees human life and relationships as mere accidents of biology and history. Its social relations are instrumentalized and regulated by the norms of contract law. The key ethical concepts become consent and consideration, rather than goodness, integrity, or virtue. As John Paul II explained in a speech delivered to the professors of Lublin University, the view of the human person derived from eighteenth-century philosophies ushers in not only Nietzsche's issue of the death of God but also the prospects of the death of man, who, in such a materialistic vision of reality, does not have any possibilities in the final eschatological sense other than those objects of the visible order. In short, in the culture of death, the human person becomes a commodity.

Alternatively, for John Paul II, the civilization of love needed to be built on the recognition that "Jesus Christ, the Redeemer of Man, is the centre and purpose of human history." The principle enunciated in this first sentence of his first encyclical, *Redemptor Hominis*, was widely regarded as his shot across the bow of the Marxists, for whom the first sentence of Karl Marx's *Communist Manifesto* offered the theory that the dynamic of world history is class struggle.

John Paul II's intensely Christocentric understanding of history is evident in his frequent references to §22 of *Gaudium et Spes*, the Second Vatican Council's Pastoral Constitution on the Church in the Modern World. That section begins with the following statement: "The truth is that only in the mystery of the incarnate Word does the mystery of man take on light. For Adam, the first man, was a figure of Him who was to come, namely Christ the Lord. Christ, the final Adam, by the revelation of the mystery of the Father, and His Love, fully reveals man to man himself and makes his supreme calling clear. It is not surprising then, that in Him all the aforementioned truths find their root and attain their crown."

This theme was reiterated in his encyclicals on God the Father, *Dives in Misericordia* (1980), and on God the Holy Spirit, *Dominum et Vivificantem* (1986). These three encyclicals—*Redemptor Hominis*, *Dives in Misericordia*, and *Dominum et Vivificantem*—formed a triptych, with each one focused on a different person of the Trinity and that particular divine Person's mission in the lives of human persons. In §50 of *Dominum et Vivificantem*, John Paul II wrote: "The Incarnation of God the Son signifies the taking up into unity with God not only of human nature, but in this human nature, in a sense, of everything that is 'flesh': the whole of humanity, the entire visible world and material world." However, in the same encyclical, he also observed: "The resistance to the Holy Spirit which St. Paul emphasizes in the interior and subjective dimension as tension, struggle and rebellion taking place in the human heart finds in every period of history, and especially in the modern era, its external dimension, which takes concrete form as the content of culture and civilization, as a philosophical system, an ideology, a program for action and for shaping human behavior."

Thus, while cultures understood in the *Kultur* sense have the potential to be epiphanies of God's glory, the philosophical and theological principles that give them form can make them inept or even hostile to any attempt of the Church to mediate the grace of the Incarnation to the world. An International Theological Commission document drafted when Cardinal Ratzinger was the ITC Chairman expressed the problem in the following way:

> In the last times inaugurated at Pentecost, the risen Christ, Alpha and Omega, enters into the history of peoples: from that moment, the sense of history and thus of culture is unsealed and the Holy Spirit reveals it by actualizing and communicating it to all. The Church is the sacrament of this revelation and its communication. It re-centers every culture into which Christ is received, placing it in the axis of the "world which is coming" and restores the union broken by the "Prince of this world." Culture is thus eschatologically situated; it tends towards its completion in Christ,

but it cannot be saved except by associating itself with the repudiation of evil.[2]

The culture of death is thus one whose foundational principles resist this re-centering on Christ and the world that is to come, and instead, like the Prince of this world, it prefers the goods of the tree of knowledge of good and evil to those of the tree of life.

Proponents of the principles that undergird the culture of death usually agree with Friedrich Nietzsche that Christianity is a crime against life itself. They regard Christianity as a religion built upon the resentment nurtured by the weak and applied to fettering the freedoms of the strong and talented, especially their sexual freedom. In 1888, Nietzsche wrote: "The assault against Christianity has not only been fainthearted, it has been wide of the mark. So long as Christian ethics are not felt to be a capital crime against life, their defenders will have the game in their hands. The problem of the 'truth' of Christianity . . . is in itself a very subsidiary problem so long as the value of Christian ethics goes unquestioned."[3] As we all know, some eighty years later the notion that Christian ethics are "a crime against life itself" was widely promoted by the intellectual elite of the generation of 1968. The social influence of this elite has been of such a magnitude that sociologists have coined the expression the *soixante-huitards* to refer to them.

Many of the encyclicals of the pontificate of John Paul II, but particularly *Veritatis Splendor* (1993) and *Evangelium Vitae* (1995), offered critiques of the alternative moral frameworks of the generation of '68. These frameworks included economism (the idea of subordinating all ethical decisions to the tribunal of economic growth and efficiency), consequentialism (the denial that human actions have any inherent moral qualities aside from their possible consequences or secondary effects), and utilitarianism (the notion that the best moral actions are those that have a favorable outcome for the majority of people affected by them).

Each of these critiques is related both to the infrastructural principles of Western culture understood as a civilization and to particular practices within institutions. For example, a hospital run on economist and utili-

---

[2] International Theological Commission, "Faith and Inculturation" (1988), §28, accessed March 22, 2017, http://www.vatican.va/roman_curia/congregations/cfaith/cti_documents/rc_cti_1988_fede-inculturazione_en.html.

[3] Friedrich Nietzsche as quoted by Henri de Lubac in *The Drama of Atheistic Humanism* (San Francisco: Ignatius Press, 1995), 115.

tarian principles is vastly different in its ethos from a hospital run on the Christian principles that every life holds the same value as every other life, that there are higher goods than economic efficiency, and that sick people are patients to be treated as if they were Christ Himself, not clients consuming a product.

Of all the institutions at risk of being subsumed by the culture of death, the one that was highest on the Pope's list of concern was that of the family. He regarded the family as the primary battlefield in which the war for the soul of Western culture was taking place. In many of his homilies, he referred to the family as the "domestic church."

Since the University of St. Thomas in Houston was founded by the Basilian fathers, and since Archbishop Miller is a member of the Basilian Order, it might be appropriate to offer as an example of what John Paul II meant by a domestic church, the family of St. Basil the Great (329–379). The entry in the *New Catholic Encyclopedia* begins by relating that St. Basil the Elder, the father of St. Basil the Great, was the son of a Christian and his wife Macrina, both of whom suffered for the faith during the persecution of Galerius which lasted from 305 until 314. St. Basil the Elder married Emmelia, the daughter of a martyr, and together they had ten children, five of whom are now venerated as saints, including St. Basil the Great. St. Basil and his siblings were homeschooled by their father and grandmother.

While it is not necessary to have homeschooled ten children, five of whom become venerated as saints, in order to qualify for Pope John Paul's "domestic church" status, the general idea is that the culture of the family understood in the sense of *Geist* or ethos is the seedbed of the faith and the front line of resistance to the forces of militant secularism. It is within the intimacy of family life that a spiritual disposition in favor of life and love over power and pragmatism is best fostered. However, one of the problems many families face is that contemporary Western culture is so geared toward the pursuit of power and other Nietzschean virtues that, in order to nurture the faith of children, it is often necessary to critique the wider culture for them and to tell them that what many people regard as normal is not, in fact, normal, but to do so in such a way that one does not ultimately produce social misfits. A certain amount of social adaptability is a survival skill most parents would want their children to acquire. Bringing up children so that they are in the world but not of the world is a difficult task requiring extraordinary prudential judgment.

It is at this point that we confront the issue of the self-development of individuals, or what the Germans called *Bildung*, and therefore, at this point that we leave the pontificate of John Paul II and move on to the treatment of culture in the sense of self-development in the thought of Joseph Ratzinger/Pope Benedict XVI.

Whereas, before becoming John Paul II, Karol Wojtyła spent the early years of his priesthood fighting the Old Left, hard-core Stalinists and the like who were true believers in dialectical materialism and obsessed with the class struggle, Ratzinger returned from the Second Vatican Council in 1965 to encounter the New Left in the German universities. The New Left was more interested in human emotions than dialectics and more interested in sex than the class struggle. As a Professor at the University of Tübingen, the young Fr. Ratzinger found himself close to the epicenter of the cultural revolution of the *soixante-huitards*. While some of his fellow priests handed out communion to Marxist students manning the picket lines around the Sorbonne, in effect forging some kind of Catholic–New Left alliance, Ratzinger's response was to regard the student revolution as just another in a series of secular humanist attempts to find meaning in the world without God. He therefore stood opposed to the pastoral strategies of many of his colleagues to effect a reconciliation between the Church and the spirit of the 1960s.

As it is generally known, in the mid-to-late 1960s, Ratzinger was a member of the editorial board of the theology journal *Concilium*, to which many of his fellow *periti* from the Second Vatican Council contributed. However, at the *Concilium* conference held in Brussels in 1970, it was quite clear that there was no common interpretation of the documents of the Second Vatican Council held by the former *periti*. Quite significant intellectual divisions had developed within the group. Ratzinger left the board of *Concilium*, and in 1972, he cofounded an alternative journal named *Communio* with Hans Urs von Balthasar and Henri de Lubac. In shorthand terms, it is said that *Concilium* became the flagship for interpretations of the Second Vatican Council that used a hermeneutic of rupture and *Communio* became the flagship for interpretations based on a hermeneutic of continuity. For the *Communio* theologians, 1965 was not a theological year zero. In 1972, Ratzinger was very much the junior member of the *Communio* set, and he has subsequently written that he "cannot even begin to say" how much he owes to his encounter with Balthasar and de Lubac.

A significant theme in Balthasar's work that influenced Ratzinger's understanding of culture as *Bildung* or self-development is the notion that, since the period of the Renaissance, the *perichoretic* (circumincessive) relationship between truth, beauty, and goodness has been severed. In philosophical thought, truth no longer has anything to do with beauty and goodness, beauty no longer has anything to do with truth and goodness, and goodness no longer has anything to do with truth and beauty. Balthasar believed that, in the culture of modernity, it is often difficult for people to see the truth or be attracted to goodness because of this severance.

Ratzinger accepts this Balthasarian insight and adds to it the argument that not only have the transcendentals been separated from their *perichoretic* relationship, but the theological virtues of faith, hope, and love have been both severed and mutated. Ratzinger observes that people still have faith, they still have hope, and they continue to regard love as a good thing. But their faith is now more in scientific reason than it is in Christ; their hope is more in scientific and material progress than it is in our redemption won by Christ; and love is usually reduced to *eros* severed from any relationship to *agape*.

So, one might say that the underlying framework for Ratzinger's account of culture as self-development or *Bildung* is provided by his understanding of the work of the transcendental properties of being (truth, beauty, and goodness) and the work of the theological virtues (faith, hope, and love). Self-development requires that the faculties of the soul—the intellect, the will, and the memory—are receptive to the theological virtues and participate in the transcendental properties. If, in the culture understood as *Kultur* or *Geist*, the transcendental properties have been severed and the theological virtues mutated, then it becomes difficult for those immersed in such cultures to rise above them.

These issues of the severance of the *perichoretic* relationship between truth, beauty, and goodness and the secularist mutations of the theological virtues are only two aspects of the much larger problem that is identified by Ratzinger in his *Principles of Catholic Theology* (1982) as the fundamental theological crisis of our age. This he defined as "coming to an understanding of the mediation of history in the realm of ontology."[4] He believes that history becomes problematical when a particular culture understood in the *Kultur*/civilization sense is in a state of crisis. The dramatic change in historical context fosters an awareness of the multitude of different lifestyle options and raises questions about whether there is any normativity in nature.

In the intellectual world, this crisis of providing an understanding of the mediation of history in the realm of ontology was fueled by the publication of Martin Heidegger's *Being and Time* in 1927. Heidegger accused

---

[4]   Joseph Ratzinger, *Principles of Catholic Theology* (San Francisco: Ignatius, 1987), 160.

the whole Scholastic tradition of neglecting the historical dimension in human identity, which criticism was in turn the intellectual impetus for the existentialist movement, and the trauma occasioned by two world wars and an economic depression was the social impetus for that movement. Both the young Wojtyła and the young Ratzinger were influenced by this Heideggerian criticism of preconciliar Scholasticism. Wojtyła responded by developing the Thomist tradition in a personalist direction, while the young Ratzinger responded by returning to the theology of St. Augustine and working on the development of an Augustinian personalism.

Both argued that, while Heidegger was correct to criticize preconciliar Scholasticism for its neglect of history—and thus, one might add, of culture—they did not agree with Heidegger's wholesale abandonment of Thomist metaphysics. For both, the human person is defined by substantiality, or one might say the human hardware created by God (what is usually called "human nature"), which is universal, as well as by relationality, or one might say the human software, those relationships that make us unique individuals, unique beings in time (which is itself particular). Ratzinger has written that the era of defining the human person solely in terms of substantiality is over, but he still believes that the dimension of substantiality is absolutely fundamental and cannot be abandoned.

Unfortunately, in *Principles of Catholic Theology*, Ratzinger did not attend to the task of providing his own definitive account of the mediation of history in the realm of ontology, though he did argue that Karl Rahner's attempt to deal with the issue in *Hearers of the Word* (first published in 1941) made the mistake of making man's being itself historical in character: "Rahner appropriated universal reason for Christianity and tried to prove that universal reason leads ultimately to the teachings of Christianity and that the teachings of Christianity are the universally human, the rational par excellence. In the generation that followed Rahner the direction of his thought was reversed. If the teachings of Christianity are the universally human, the generally held views are what is Christian. If that is the case, then one must interpret what is Christian in terms of the universal findings of man's reason."[5]

Thus, in some parts of the world, one ended up with Catholic academics promoting liberation theology because Marxism was seen by some at least to be the most rational account of human social reality, while other Catholic academics sought to criticize Catholic moral teaching on the grounds that it did not accord with other contemporary movements in

---

[5] Ibid., 168.

philosophy or with feminist social theory. Proponents of the hermeneutic of rupture approach to the Second Vatican Council often take the view that the central meaning of the Council was the inauguration of a general openness to philosophical currents in the world at large. The position of Ratzinger and his *Communio* colleagues was that this was not the central message of Vatican II and that, in any case, any such openness must always be accompanied by a critical reading of new philosophical movements with reference to Revelation.

One might conclude this section by saying that Ratzinger's account of *Bildung*/self-development is based on the notion that God and the human person are in a dialogical relationship in which prayer and the sacraments are the primary modes of communication and in which the work of the theological virtues and the transcendental properties of truth, beauty, and goodness is central. One might also conclude that, in various ways, a significant difference between Ratzinger and Rahner (a leading proponent of the hermeneutic of rupture) was their attitude toward a specifically Catholic culture. Ratzinger's orientation is to foster what he calls "the culture of the Incarnation," whereas Rahner and the great majority of theologians of his generation regarded the culture of modernity as something that is here to stay and to which Catholics needed to accommodate themselves.

In the theology journals, the notion that the Catholic faith needed to be repackaged in contemporary idioms and practices went by the label of "correlationism." The idea, when popularized, was that Catholic elites needed to correlate the faith to trends in popular culture. One was to pick up on certain cultural trends and concepts that were popular and try to tie the Catholic faith to them, and the idea of there being a specifically Catholic culture was rejected and associated with a ghetto mentality. Ratzinger criticized such pastoral strategies in the following terms: "One might think that the culture is the affair of the individual historical country while faith for its part is in search of cultural expression. The individual cultures would allocate, as it were, a cultural body to the faith. Accordingly, faith would always have to live from borrowed cultures, which remain in the end somehow external and capable of being cast off. . . . Such thinking is at root Manichean. Culture is debased, becoming a mere exchangeable shell and faith is reduced to a disincarnated spirit ultimately void of reality."[6] He went on to say that, if culture is more than a mere form

---

6   Joseph Ratzinger, "Christ, Faith and the Challenge of Cultures," Address to the Presidents of the Asian Bishops Conferences, Hong Kong, March 2–5, 1993, accessed March 13, 2017, http://www.ewtn.com/library/CURIA/RATZHONG.HTM.

or aesthetic principle, if it is rather the ordering of values in an historical living form, and if it cannot prescind from the question of God, then we cannot circumvent the fact that the Church is her own cultural subject for the faithful.

Rather than correlating the Catholic faith to the culture of modernity, Ratzinger/Benedict thinks that the culture of the Catholic faith itself should challenge the contemporary nihilist culture of death. For taking this stance, the *soixante-huitards* regard him as a reactionary. Somewhat less academically, they have also called him a snob. This is in part because of his criticism of the rock music industry, its cults of narrative-wreck celebrities, and the general effect of contemporary pop culture on the formation of youth. He regards rock music as a regression to the paganism of the Dionysian cults in classical Greece.

Most pop-culture celebrities are not only post-Christian but their lives are often what philosophers call "narrative wrecks." The narrative or story of their life contains so many twists and contradictions that their personal integrity has been shattered. They often employ an entourage of "minders," including life coaches, to advise them on how to conduct their professional and private affairs. Whereas the life of an ordinary Christian is described in the sociology journals as a life "celebrated recurrence" in which certain feast days and liturgies are celebrated the same way year after year and in which there is only one model of a perfected humanity, that of Jesus Christ, the lifestyle that was celebrated by the elite of the generation of '68 was one that gave priority to originality and difference. The more original the lifestyle, the greater its difference from that of an ordinary person, the more likely a person was to qualify for celebrity status. Lifestyles became works of art. Although they were supposed to be self-constructed without reference to any external standard, often the individuals who qualified for celebrity status became products. Far from controlling their own lifestyle choices, they were packaged and marketed by their managers.

For Ratzinger, then, the pop culture industry is an important component of John Paul II's culture of death because it retards the spiritual development of youth. He is therefore critical of those pastoral strategies, often found in secondary schools and youth ministries, of making the faith fashionable by correlating or tying it to the pop-culture industry.

Yves de Maeseneer has written a fascinating essay comparing the reception of the stigmata by St. Francis of Assisi with the mechanisms by which brand logos are engraved on the human memory and form an element of contemporary youth culture. He develops the thesis that brand-name multinational corporations have their own theo-aesthetic program.[7] According to Naomi Klein, author of the best-selling book *No Logo*, the brand-name multinational corporations sell images and lifestyles rather than simple commodities: "Branding is about ideas, attitudes, lifestyle and values all embodied in the logo." The market power of brands and logos associated with international celebrity figures attests to a sublimated need in secular culture for the sacramental, that is, for signs, symbols, and even grace that help to define the self. The contemporary popularity of "body art" tattoos may well be attesting to the same need to fill the "hole," so to speak, left by the erosion of a sacramental cosmos and especially the failure of post-Christian parents to have their children baptized.

Pope Benedict not only implores Christians not to buy into the culture of a secularist substitute for sacramentality but also positively tries to defend and promote the Christian belief in the true, the beautiful, and the good as transcendental properties of being and belief in the theological virtues of faith, hope, and love as an alternative theoretical foundation for self-development. The transcendental properties of truth, beauty, and goodness are linked to the theological virtues of faith, hope, and charity and to the faculties of the human soul—the intellect, the memory, and the will—in such a way that the theological virtue of faith works on the intellect to lead it to truth, the theological virtue of love works on the will to lead it to goodness, and the theological virtue of hope works on the memory and fosters its thirst for beauty. While aspects of contemporary mass culture are hostile to truth, beauty, and goodness, it is mass culture's attack on beauty that was so central in the prepapal writings of Ratzinger.

In order for a low and increasingly secularist mass culture with its cult of celebrities to be so pervasive, the Church's own sacramental culture must be very weak. Theologians are now beginning to ask why. In his work *The Sense of the Supernatural*, Jean Borella diagnoses this loss of the sense of the supernatural as a secondary effect of the loss of the sense of the ontological. In order to have this capacity reawakened within us, Borella argues, "we need to have in this world of ours an experience of forms, which by themselves, refer to nothing of the mundane."[8] Such experiences are given to us by liturgical forms, that is, by symbols through which the invisible transcendent renders itself more visible. Borella ac-

---

[7] Yves de Maeseneer, "St. Francis versus McDonalds: Contemporary Globalization Critique and Hans Urs von Balthasar's Theological Aesthetics," *Heythrop Journal* 44, no. 1 (2003): 1–14.

[8] Jean Borella, *The Sense of the Supernatural* (London: T & T Clark, 1998), 59.

knowledges that these elements are, of course, borrowed from the physical world—"otherwise no human experience of it would be possible—but they are set aside, separated from the natural order to which they originally belonged and to which they refer, and consecrated in order to render present realities of another order."[9] These forms became the realm of the sacred, and the realm of the sacred becomes the mediator between the natural and supernatural orders.

Borella goes on to explain that sacred forms are not mediatory by themselves. They realize their mediatory function only if they are "full of grace," only if they serve as a mode of expression for the ritual activity by which the first mediation, that of the divine activity of Christ, is rendered present among us. Thus, Borella concludes, "sacred forms are tertiary mediations with our need for them dependent on ritual activity which is itself dependent on the divine activity of the crucified Mediator."[10] Nothing could be more hostile to this account of sacramentality than liturgical practices that focus on the mundane, on the secular world, and on human creativity.

Borella and Ratzinger are very much on the same page in terms of their analysis of what went wrong with the post-conciliar pastoral strategies. The idea of a self-constructed liturgy to bring God down to the level of the people and make him relevant to events in the mundane order has been described by Ratzinger as nothing less than a form of apostasy analogous to the Hebrew's worship of the Golden Calf.[11] Not only should liturgy not focus on the mundane, but in his apostolic exhortation *Sacramentum Caritatis*, Benedict stated that absolutely everything associated with the Eucharistic liturgies must be marked by beauty. He has also noted that this means that seminaries must be places of cultural formation. Seminarians need to study not only theology and philosophy but also literature, music, and history, too. He concedes that "no one can do everything," but he says, "we must not surrender to philistinism." Liturgy, he states, is the encounter with the beautiful itself, with eternal love, and therefore we have to at least strive to make it beautiful.

While John Paul II and Benedict XVI's readings of what is wrong with contemporary Western culture are not always well-received by contemporary intellectual elites and are certainly opposed by the *soixante-huitards*, they are, in effect, affirmed in Alexander Boot's book *How the West Was*

---

9   Ibid.
10   Ibid., 60.
11   Joseph Ratzinger, *The Spirit of the Liturgy* (San Francisco: Ignatius Press, 2000), 22–23.

Lost.[12] Boot traces the emergence of modern man, whom he calls "Modman," back to the Reformation, with its antihierarchical forces, and contrasts Modman with the Catholic Westman. According to Boot, Modman, an evolutionary development from Reformation man, today comes in two species: Modman Philistine and Modman Nihilist. The central message of Boot's book is that the only resistance to philistinism and nihilism within contemporary Western culture is coming from the Catholic Church and her intellectuals who understand that the main weapon of Modman is the "slow imposition of philistine values on society," accompanied by a gradual imposition of political and economic power that can force "Westman" into compliance. Included within the strategy are the replacement of the historic role of the father by the state bureaucracy and the eventual abolition of the family itself. Ratzinger's concerns about philistines being in charge of seminary formation are consistent with Boot's sociological diagnosis. A priest who is himself unable to rise above the level of mass culture will not be able to liberate others, and he will be rejected by those of a nihilist disposition as a typical member of the herd from which the nihilist is trying to escape. The Catholic Church cannot accept the judgment of Friedrich Nietzsche that Christianity is the religion of the herd.

Although his attacks on Christianity are much more indirect than those of Modman Nihilist, Modman Philistine is often more effective than Modman Nihilist precisely because the form of the attack is much more subtle. At its most general, it is an attack on the notion of excellence, on the very idea that there can be gradations of goodness and prototypical ways of being. It is for this reason that Benedict concludes that the strategy of correlating the faith to the norms of mass culture is not a new inculturation, but rather "a denial of its [the Church's] culture and prostitution with the nonculture."[13] As stated above, his solution is for us to promote the self-development of the human person with reference to the theological virtues of faith, hope, and love and the transcendental properties of truth, beauty, and goodness.

In relation to the latter, the Franciscan psychologist Benedict Groeschel has argued that most people have a primary attraction to one or another of the transcendentals. He offers St. Augustine as an example of someone whose primary transcendental was beauty, St. Thomas Aquinas as someone whose primary transcendental was truth, and St. Francis of

---

[12] Alexander Boot, *How the West Was Lost* (London: I. B. Tauris, 2006).

[13] Joseph Ratzinger, *A New Song for the Lord: Faith in Christ and Liturgy Today* (New York: Crossroad, 1996), 109.

Assisi as someone whose primary transcendental was goodness. This is not to suggest that any of these saints lacked an appreciation of the other two transcendentals, but merely that, in their work, one can detect a primary attraction to one or other of them. No one transcendental is any more important than any other, just as no member of the Trinity is more important than any other.

My guess is that St. John Paul II's primary transcendental was either truth or goodness, whereas Benedict's is clearly beauty. This means that the two papacies complemented one another by dealing with different areas of Church life in need of repair. It explains, for example, John Paul II's interest in moral theology and Benedict's interest in liturgy. Both have stood opposed to the Modman Nihilist and his culture of death. Benedict has enriched John Paul II's critique by adding to it an account of the role of Modman Philistine and his entrapment of successive generations of Catholic youth in the pseudosacramentality of celebrity pop culture. Both believe that, in the crisis of culture we are experiencing, identified by Paul VI as early as 1964, it is only from islands of spiritual concentration that a new cultural purification and unification can break out. Mass culture, with its cult of narrative-wreck celebrities and its confusion about the very meaning of love, needs to be interrupted by a high sacramental culture based on the notion that Jesus Christ, the Redeemer of Man, is the center and purpose of human history. This is the basis of what Pope Benedict has called the humanist culture of the Incarnation, which we find expounded most eloquently in John Paul II's Trinitarian triptych of encyclicals.

CHAPTER 6

Poland and Communism (for Those Too Young to Remember!)[1]

IN THE TWENTIETH CENTURY, Communist governments were responsible for the death of some 94 million people. This can be broken down into: 65 million in China, 20 million in the Soviet Union, 2 million in Cambodia, 2 million in North Korea, 1.7 million in Africa, 1.5 million in Afghanistan, 1 million in the Communist states of Eastern Europe, 1 million in Vietnam, 150,000 in Latin America, and some 10,000 deaths "resulting from actions of the international Communist movement and Communist parties not in power."[2] These statistics include the intentional destruction of whole populations by starvation and deaths resulting from deportations, physical confinement, and forced labor.

Communism was a form of government built on the ideology of the nineteenth-century German philosopher Karl Marx. The opening exhortation of his most famous book, *The Communist Manifesto*, was for the workers of the world to unite, the history of the world is the history of class struggle. His general thesis was that class struggle is the driver of human history: progress comes about when technological development gives rise to new social classes that overthrow the previously dominant social class. Just as the European bourgeoisie rose to power with the industrial revolution and overthrew the old aristocratic order, Marx predicted a new

---

[1]   Lecture given to Australian World Youth Day Pilgrims before their departure for Poland in 2016.

[2]   These statistics can be found in a number of places and are a conservative estimate. Some authorities claim that the figure is closer to 100 million than 94 million. See, for example, reason.com/blog/2013/03/13/communism-killed-94M-in-20th-century.

stage in which the industrial proletariat would wage a class war against the bourgeoisie, eliminate all private property, and give birth to a new social order called Communism. This was to be the highest stage in human development, a purely classless society in which it would be possible for people to hunt in the morning, fish after lunch, rear cattle in the evening, and philosophize after dinner.

Marx was also an atheist who had been influenced by the ideas of another nineteenth-century German, Ludwig Feuerbach. Feuerbach argued that belief in God is a psychological crutch: humans create a god for themselves because they cannot cope with the thought that there is nothing beyond death. Marx believed that it would be necessary to free the proletarian workers of their attachment to God if they were to perform their historic role of waging a successful class war against the bourgeoisie and bringing the order of Communism to life. Class war and atheism were therefore the two signature tunes of the Communists.

In the early twentieth century, Marx's ideas became popular with Russian revolutionaries who, in October of 1917, murdered the Russian royal family and effected a military coup under the leadership of Vladimir Lenin. This is usually known as the Russian Revolution or the Bolshevik Revolution, since the name "Bolshevik," meaning "the majority" in Russian, was the name chosen by the revolutionaries to describe themselves. Following a series of wars between the Bolsheviks, known also as the "reds," and their enemies, the "whites," a number of neighboring countries were annexed under Bolshevik control. What was Russia became the Union of Soviet Socialist Republics, or the USSR, or the Soviet Union for short. Within the USSR, the practice of religion was suppressed, churches were destroyed, and atheism and Marxist ideology were taught in all the schools. Those who spoke out against this found themselves in concentration camps known as gulags.

One of those neighboring lands the Red Army tried to conquer was Poland. The Red Army initially invaded Poland in 1918 but was defeated in 1920 on the Feast of the Assumption. This Polish victory is known as the Battle of Warsaw, or sometimes, more poetically, the Miracle at the Wisła (the Wisła is the river that runs through the center of Warsaw).

No one expected the Poles to see off the Red Army. So certain were foreign powers of a Polish defeat that all the embassies in Warsaw withdrew their personnel except the Holy See. The papal nuncio, Monsignor Achille Ratti, the future Pope Pius XI, remained at his post. Pope Benedict XV called on Catholics throughout the world to pray for the Poles and, on August 6, 1920, the Poles themselves began a novena to Our Lady.

Nine days later, on the Feast of the Assumption, they not only defeated but actually routed the Red Army, and the Polish people were left unmolested by the Soviets for another nineteen years.

In the accounts of the Battle of Warsaw, reference is always made to the fact that troops on both sides believed that they were seeing visions of Our Lady in the sky, and it is agreed that this made the Poles fight harder and that it scared the Bolsheviks. It is also acknowledged that the Polish General Jozef Piłsudski was tactically brilliant. His forces crept up on the Soviets from behind. The capture of Soviet code books was also of enormous assistance to the Polish strategists. After the victory, Pope Benedict XV wrote a letter to the Primate of Poland saying that the power of prayer had saved "the rampart of Europe, all Christianity, and civilization."[3]

The Bolsheviks returned to Russia defeated, but one strange historical fact is that they took with them the body of the Jesuit saint Andrew Bobola. They stole Bobola's body from a church in Warsaw and took it back to Moscow for medical analysis, since he is one of those saints whose body remains uncorrupted. Vatican diplomats did eventually retrieve it.

A couple of months before the Battle of Warsaw, on May 18, 1920, Karol Wojtyła was born to a Polish officer and his wife. They named him Karol after Emperor Karl of Austria-Hungary, in whose army his father served. He grew up to become Pope John Paul II, and in 2004, he presided at the beatification ceremony of his namesake, Emperor Karl.

On September 1, 1939, when Wojtyła was just nineteen years old, Poland was invaded from the west by Nazi Germany, and on September 17, some two weeks later, from the east by the Soviets. On October 8, Germany annexed western Poland and the former free city of Danzig, now known as Gdańsk, while at the same time, the Soviet Union immediately started a campaign of sovietization of its newly acquired areas in the east. This included staged elections, the results of which were used to legitimize the Soviet Union's annexation of eastern Poland. In April and May of 1940, some 22,000 Poles were executed by Soviet forces in what is now called the Katyn Forest massacres. This included some 8,000 Polish military officers, 6,000 Polish police officers, and 8,000 victims classified as members of the Polish intelligentsia, which naturally included many priests. Some significant numbers of Polish officers did manage to escape to Britain, where they joined up with British forces and contributed to the British

---

[3] Christopher Zugger, *The Forgotten: Catholics of the Soviet Empire from Lenin through Stalin* (Syracuse, NY: Syracuse University Press, 2001), 121.

107

defeat of the German air force. They also helped with the development of the Royal Navy's sonar system for submarines.

Britain in fact joined the Second World War because of the Nazi invasion of Poland, but at a conference in the Crimean town of Yalta in 1945, the Soviet leader Joseph Stalin, the British leader Winston Churchill, and the US President Franklin D. Roosevelt agreed that, after the war, Poland would become part of the Soviet bloc. It is for this reason that today Poles sometimes refer to their lavatories as the Winston Churchill.

As a result, from 1945 until 1989, Poland was a Communist country, or a captive nation, as these countries that fell on the wrong side of the Berlin Wall became known. Churchill did eventually admit that he had made a grave error, perhaps his biggest since Gallipoli in the First World War. A year after the Yalta Agreement, in March 1946, he gave a famous speech in which he said: "From Stettin in the Baltic to Trieste in the Adriatic an iron curtain has descended across the Continent. Behind that line lie all the capitals of the ancient states of Central and Eastern Europe: Warsaw, Berlin, Prague, Vienna, Budapest, Belgrade, Bucharest and Sofia; all these famous cities and the populations around them lie in what I must call the Soviet sphere, and all are subject, in one form or another, not only to Soviet influence but to a very high and in some cases increasing measure of control from Moscow." Karol Wojtyła found himself on this captive side of the Iron Curtain. In 1946 he was ordained to the priesthood, in 1964 he became the Archbishop of Krakow, and in 1978 he became Pope John Paul II.

At the time of his election to the papacy, the Polish Communist government was preparing a propaganda campaign about a Polish cosmonaut who had been working with the Soviet space program. They were intending to highlight the benefits of the Polish relationship with the Soviets by reference to how good it was to have a cosmonaut as a national icon. But the election of a Polish pope ended all of that; Wojtyła eclipsed the cosmonaut.

As the cardinals went forward to congratulate the new pope and one by one fell to their knees and kissed his ring, the Polish people were treated to the spectacle of the new pontiff himself falling to his knees to embrace the Cardinal Archbishop of Warsaw, Stefan Wyszyński. Wyszyński had been a prisoner of the Communists between 1953 and 1956. The achievement for which he is most famous is that of organizing the "Great Novena," a nine-year-long program of Catholic devotions in preparation for the celebration of one thousand years of Polish Christianity in the year 1966. Throughout the period of the Great Novena, Wyszyński was constantly doing battle with Communist authorities who tried to stop processions and pilgrimages, especially to the shrine of the Black Madonna at Częstochowa. He responded to the Communist tactics by deciding that if the people could not go to Częstochowa, then the sacred image of the Black Madonna would go to the people. When the Communists set up road blocks around Częstochowa to prevent the image of the Black Madonna from leaving the monastery and being taken on tour through Polish towns and villages, Wyszyński ordered an empty picture frame to be taken on tour which served as a dramatic illustration of the stupidity of the Communists.

It is difficult, therefore, to overstate how dramatic a moment in world history it was when a newly elected Polish pope moved from the Chair of Peter to kneel before his old battle-scarred lion. It was a gesture that spoke volumes to the millions of Poles watching it on television. Suddenly the Poles were no longer a wretched bunch of people sandwiched between Communist-controlled East Germany on the one side and the Communist Ukraine on the other, a nation demoralized by its loss of the best and brightest of a generation, its betrayal by the Western powers, and its impotence to defend itself against the Soviets. Poland now had an advocate on the world stage and one who had a particularly charming personality who had turned down a career as an actor to become a priest. If his *Wikipedia* entry is to be believed, he could speak some fourteen languages, which is a major diplomatic asset.

To use a Harry Potter metaphor, the Communists operated like dementors: they sucked the hope out of people. No individual could stand against them and win. It would take an entire nation to collectively resist, and after the horror of World War II and their ultimate betrayal by the leaders of the United Kingdom and the United States, and after spending hours of every day standing in food queues and living with three generations in two-bedroom apartments and all the other conditions that went with Communism, including a constant shortage of medicines and toilet paper, the Polish people did not have the strength to stand against the entire might of the Soviet Union. There is an old joke: When Vladimir Lenin died, tens of thousands of Russians lined the snow-covered streets of Moscow and slowly progressed toward his coffin; when a journalist asked them why, they said, "We have heard that a fresh cabbage has just come in from Helsinki." That joke rather sums up life in a Communist country. People were constantly ground down by the ordeal of daily survival. The election of Wojtyła to the papacy gave the Polish people hope. They stopped feeling abandoned and powerless. In June of 1979, John Paul II returned to Poland on an official nine-day papal visit and literally millions of Poles listened to his every speech and took to heart his message of "Be Not Afraid."

This exhortation spurred the generation who had grown up during the period of the Great Novena to action. In September 1980, the first free trade union movement was established inside the Soviet bloc, known as *Solidarność*, or Solidarity, under the leadership of Lech Wałesa, an electrician from the Gdańsk shipyard. A year later, this free (non-Communist) trade union was suppressed following a declaration of martial law. This action by Polish Communist officials (the declaration of martial law) led to pro-Solidarity street demonstrations across Western Europe and the countries of the British Commonwealth, as well as in parts of the United States with large populations of people with Polish ancestry, such as Chicago and Philadelphia. Trade unionists, Polish emigres, Catholics of all ethnic backgrounds, and young university students marched behind banners bearing the words "Let Poland be Poland." At this time, Margaret Thatcher was Prime Minister of England and Ronald Reagan had just been elected President of the United States. Both were strongly anti-Communist. The US State Department under Reagan shared diplomatic intelligence with the Vatican, and there followed some eight years of political struggle between the Communists and their political opponents. Contending with Soviet political puppets was no longer an isolated Polish fight. Under John Paul II's leadership, it became fashionable for people outside Polish circles to champion the efforts of Solidarity to make Poland a free country.

On May 13, 1981, John Paul II survived an assassination attempt by a Turkish gunman who had links to the Bulgarian secret police. He was on his way to open the first John Paul II Institute for Marriage and Family at the Pontifical Lateran University when the shooting took place. Although the KGB denied any involvement, it is widely believed that the Soviet government was using one of its surrogates to rid itself of the problem of an anti-Communist Polish pope.

John Paul II survived the assassination attempt and attributed his recovery to Our Lady of Fatima. The bullet seemed to change its trajectory and miraculously miss vital organs as it entered the pope's body. When his postoperative care was not going well, a medical professor at the University of Edinburgh spoke to one of the Dominican chaplains at the University and suggested a different course of action. The Dominican put the professor in contact with the pope's doctors through the papal nuncio's office, his advice was adopted, and John Paul II recovered.

In October of 1984, Fr. Jerzy Popiełuszko, one of the most significant spiritual leaders of the Solidarity movement, was murdered by agents of the secret police. Some 250,000 people attended his funeral, and this act made the Communist authorities even less popular internally and abroad (Fr. Popiełuszko has since been beatified by Benedict XVI).

The Poles finally achieved freedom in August of 1989 when the Communists permitted Tadeusz Mazowiecki, a member of Solidarity, to take over as Prime Minister. The fall of Communism in Poland had a domino effect in neighboring captive nations, and the Berlin Wall—the starkest symbol of the Iron Curtain—was itself torn down on November 9, 1989. Mikhail Gorbachev, the last of the Soviet leaders, was later to say that "the collapse of the Iron Curtain would have been impossible without John Paul II."

The Contribution of the Polish Intelligentsia to the Breakthrough of 1989[1]

IN HIS RECOLLECTIONS of the events of June 1979, the former Solidarity advisor Adam Michnik has described this moment in history as a time of three Polish miracles. First, John Paul II returned triumphantly to Poland as a pope, making a mockery of Stalin's jibe about the pope having no divisions. Then the second miracle occurred a little over a year later in the August of 1980 when Lech Wałęsa led the shipyard's strike and the first non-Communist trade union was formed within the Soviet bloc. The third miracle happened some two months later when the exiled poet Czesław Miłosz was awarded the Nobel Prize for literature. Michnik wrote:

> John Paul II became the emblem of Poland's Catholic Church at its best. The Gdansk strike and Lech Wałęsa became symbols and the crowning point of the Polish workers' rebellion and Czesław Miłosz symbolized the defiance of Poland's intelligentsia. Those three symbols marked the three trends within Solidarity. One of them stressed the movement's national and Catholic character, another followed the working class vindication line, another still concentrated on democratic and humanist values. These tenden-

---

[1] First published in *Humanities Research of the Australian National University* 16, no. 3 (2010).

cies were neither inconsistent nor conflicting; for us they were complementary.[2]

This essay will focus on the humanist values of the Polish intelligentsia that were not only significant for the third miracle of 1980 but also greatly contributed to the final breakthrough of the summer of 1989. For a whole decade, they offered sustained intellectual critiques of really existing Marxism and reflections on the alternatives available in Western political thought. Included within this body of work were the contributions of Karol Wojtyła (Pope John Paul II), who was both a Polish intellectual and a powerful world figure.

While members of the Polish intelligentsia were offering critiques of various forms of totalitarian government from the 1930s onwards, the work of anti-Communist scholars and writers became more organized in the 1970s with the formation of the Workers Defense Committee, known by its initials KOR (*Komitet Obrony Robotników*). KOR was distinctive in that it was an initiative of intellectuals to assist workers and their families, particularly those prisoners detained after labor strikes in 1976. It raised money through the sale of its underground publications, through fund-raising groups in Paris and London, and through grants from Western institutions. KOR sent open letters of protest to the Communist government and organized legal and financial support for the families of detainees. The group also smuggled in printing machines to produce its underground publications such as *Robotnik*, a biweekly that had a circulation of around twenty thousand by 1978, and to publish books under the banner of its own publishing house, called NOWA.[3] The latter were often Polish translations of works published in other Western countries that were regarded as politically dangerous by the Communist authorities. George Orwell's *Nineteen Eighty-Four*, with its esoteric critique of the Bolshevik Revolution of 1917, and Günter Grass's *The Tin Drum* were prominent in this category. Jan Józef Lipski concluded that the achievement of NOWA was "truly impressive," with over one hundred publications, including political and economic works that were "in-

---

[2] Adam Michnik, "In Search of Lost Sense," *Signs and Sights*, September 29, 2005, accessed March 13, 2017, www.signandsight.com/features/373.html. This is the English translation of an article originally published in Polish in *Gazeta Wyborcza*, then in German translation in *Die Zeit*, September 1, 2005.

[3] Jan Józef Lipski, *KOR: A History of the Worker's Defense Committee in Poland, 1976–1981* (Berkeley, CA: University of California Press, 1985), 179.

dispensable to an understanding of intellectual and political culture."[4]

In 1977, KOR leaders collaborated with intellectuals in the Warsaw community to establish the Flying University (*Uniwersytet Latający*), which was a series of lectures organized by unofficial student groups to discuss political topics that could not be debated in public. The concept was revived from a similar organization that had operated between the years 1885 and 1905 in the context of Imperial Russia's domination of the Polish capital.[5] As a consequence of their collaboration with the organizers of the Flying University, KOR members were harassed by the secret police, beaten up, and in some cases jailed. However, KOR became an inspiration for the nation when the Polish government declared amnesty for jailed workers in the Spring of 1977. The work of KOR was thus a precursor to the formation of Solidarity. Its leading members included Jacek Kuron, Jan Jozef Lipski, and Adam Michnik.

In addition to the political agitation and publication work undertaken by KOR members, there was also a significant body of scholarship being published in the field of political theory by intellectuals not formally associated with KOR. Far from having uncritically accepted the tendency of many Western scholars to reduce the study of politics to issues in public administration, Polish scholars throughout the 1980s published essays on the entire tradition of Western political philosophy in the journals *Res Publica*, *Kontakt*, *Libertas*, *Arka*, *Wiez*, *Znak*, *Christianitas*, and *Gazeta Wyborcza* and the newspaper *Tygodnik Powszechny*. Many of these essays sought to uncover the foundations of the totalitarian mindset in the fact–value dichotomy.

In 1980, Pawel Spiewak published an essay in the journal *Wiez*, then under the editorial guidance of Tadeusz Mazowiecki, who was to become the first Solidarity Prime Minister in the summer of 1989. The article endorsed the argument of Robert Nisbet that the fundamental cleavage in modern political discourse is not between the left and the right but between those who want to separate politics from the domain of values and those who do not.[6] Those who argue that politics and values should be kept chastely separate speak of the moral neutrality of the state as a new kind of civic virtue. They reject the idea that there is a list of goods of human flourishing whose promotion and defense by the state fosters the common good.

---

[4] Ibid.

[5] Ibid., 208–10.

[6] Pawel Spiewak, "Nisbet: Filozofia pluralizmu," *Wiez* 6 (1980): 117.

Two of the leading Western political theorists of the twentieth century who wanted to distill the ether of values from the political process were professors at Harvard University. One of them, Robert Nozick, was of the view that no political action on the part of the state may be undertaken or justified on the ground that it promotes an ideal of the good or on the ground that it enables individuals to pursue an ideal of the good. Meanwhile, his colleague John Rawls thought that those who believe in concepts like the common good were "irrational" and "mad," and to underscore this principle, he said that, if a human being wants to spend his life counting blades of grass, then that is his good, and the rest of us have no grounds upon which to judge otherwise.[7]

While the idea that moral neutrality is a virtue was one of the dominant themes in late-twentieth-century Western political theory, it did not sit well with many of the Polish anti-Communist dissident intellectuals. With reference to such currents of thought in Western countries, Zdzisław Krasnodębski observed that, according to neutrality theorists, it is wrong to assume that the distinction between good and evil may be clearly discerned, to think that we could have any claim to know the whole, to be the advocate for the universal subject—and that, since nothing is morally certain, we are all simultaneously victims and executioners. All that Poland could expect from a Western culture penetrated by such ideas was something as mundane as a supermarket. He lamented that the lost paradise of Europe could not be rejoined because premodern Europe no longer exists: Western Europeans had sold their souls to utilitarian and other materialist currents of philosophy no less than the Communists. There was no archaic Ithaca to which Poland might return because Penelope (Western Europe) did not wait faithfully; she had submitted to some rather low-minded suitors.[8]

While Krasnodębski identified the problem of the moral equivocation of the West, Marcin Król, who was then the editor of the Warsaw based journal *Res Publica*, argued that Nazism was possible in the Weimar Republic precisely because many citizens of that republic no longer aspired to ideals and values that formed a bridge between politics and ethics. The sense of aimlessness, or what Max Weber described as "disenchantment," had created a moral vacuum in the political realm such

---

[7]   Robert Nozick, *Anarchy, State, and Utopia* (Oxford: Blackwell, 1984), 312; John Rawls, *A Theory of Justice* (Oxford: Clarendon, 1972), 554.

[8]   Zdzisław Krasnodębski, "W oczekiwaniu na supermarkety—czyli upadek komonizmu w swietle postmodernistycznej filozofii widziany," *Res Publica* 4 (1991): 74.

that it was difficult for the opinion-makers to make moral judgments. Król refers to the condition generated by the fact–value dichotomy as the "terrorism of the lack of ideals." He argued that the idea that human beings can make no rational judgments about values, only about facts, imported the Machiavellian separation of politics from morality, and the separation of descriptions of reality from considerations of how societies ought to be.[9]

In his article "The Problems with Machiavelli" (*Kłopoty z Machiavellim*), Król further argued that the Machiavellian error can take three forms in modern political life. First, there is the attitude that politics is always immoral and, thus, the moral citizen should avoid the political sphere altogether. Second, there is the attitude that politics is the realm of pure tactics, and thus, those operating within it are free from the operation of moral imperatives. Third, there is the attitude that moral behavior is always determined by politics, that there are always political explanations for whatever it is that we believe about values. It was this third version that was at the basis of the Marxist idea that what humans believed to be right or wrong could always be explained by their class status. According to the Communists, bourgeois morality was one thing and proletarian morality something else. Having set out the three different forms that the separation of politics from values had taken in the twentieth century, Król noted that common to all three was a denial of the human capacity for the exercise of free will.

Król concluded that, if ideas like justice, goodness, and human rights are not related to any objective reality, then one can use them at will; there is nothing to stand in opposition to their arbitrary use because there is no external and transcendental perspective. Principles of justice must not be dependent upon the state for their definition. If they are, then the state can acknowledge as law whatever it will and it may very well become not merely the executive committee of the ruling class but, even worse, the executive committee of the ruling party. Król suggested that there is much to fear from conceptions of the state that are based in a rationality that is divorced from conscience. The moment that legitimacy is founded on or confused with rational bureaucratic legality, there is a risk that legitimacy and conscience will be absorbed by the state and that ordinary citizens will exit themselves from the scene of the crime.[10]

These ideas resonated strongly with those of the Czech dissident in-

---

[9] Marcin Król, "Dylematy Liberalizmu," *Aneks* 34 (1984).
[10] Marcin Król, "Kłopoty z Machiavellim," *Lad Utajony* (Krakow: Znak, 1983), 34–36.

tellectual Václav Havel, who coined the expression "the power of the powerless." In his essay "Anti-Political Politics," Havel argued that, for all the complex historical detours, the origin of the modern state and of political power may be sought in the moment when human reason broke free of humanity, of personal experience, personal conscience, and personal responsibility, and also from the framework of the natural world. Havel observed that, in contemporary politics, "good and evil, categories of the natural world, are obsolete remnants of the past which have lost all meaning and that the sole method of politics is quantifiable success, that is, the teaching of Machiavelli."[11]

For this reason, Havel did not equate his rejection of Soviet-style Communism with an embrace of the political styles of the West. To the extent that they were based on the rational technology of power, he rejected them. In an interview with the *Times Literary Supplement*, he described Soviet totalitarianism as an "extreme manifestation of a deep-seated problem which equally finds expression in advanced Western society. Both systems, Soviet and Western liberal-democratic, have in common Belohradsky's 'eschatology of the impersonal,' the trend toward mega-machines that escape human control."[12] When asked for his analysis of the causes of the problem, Havel replied: "It has something to do with the fact that we live in the first atheistic civilization in human history. People have ceased to respect any so-called higher metaphysical values. . . . I am not talking about a personal God necessarily, I'm referring to whatever is absolute, transcendental, supra-human. These fundamental considerations once represented a support, a horizon for people, but now they are lost."[13]

Adam Michnik also addressed the subject of the Machiavellian foundations of much contemporary political theory. In 1990, one year after the breakthrough of the summer of 1989, he began an article entitled "After the Revolution: The New Dangers to the New Democracies" with the observation that many think of politics as the art of achieving what is possible in a given situation. In this respect, the consideration of what is good and what is bad, what is fair and what is unfair, what is honest and what is dishonest, is external to politics, and in this way, it can be said that politics and ethics belong to different worlds. However, with reference to Havel's concept of the power of the powerless, he then moved on from this com-

---

[11] Václav Havel, "Anti-Political Politics," in *Civil Society and the State* (London: Verso, 1988), 387–88.

[12] Václav Havel, "Doing without Utopias," *Times Literary Supplement*, January 23, 1987, 81.

[13] Ibid.

monplace observation to assert that the men and women of the anti-totalitarian opposition movements had a different view of politics:

> We are engaged in a great experiment of confrontation between the idea of politics based on the power of the powerless and a social reality that was shaped when politics was based on the power of the powerful. . . . We are children of a certain tradition. And we know that this tradition does not permit us to renounce the truth with impunity. We are the children of our Judeo-Christian culture, and we know that this culture, which recommends loyalty to the state, commands us to bend our knees only before God. We know therefore, that we should put faithfulness to truth above participation in power. We know, by reaching for our roots, that the truth of politics resides, in the end, in the politics of truth. . . . We reject the belief in political utopia. We know that our future is an imperfect society, a society of ordinary people and ordinary conflicts—but, precisely for this reason, a society that must not renounce its ethical norms in the name of political illusions.[14]

Many of the above criticisms of the quest to sever the connection between the political and the moral can be found in a more synthesized form in the works of John Paul II. For the young Karol Wojtyła, a major problem facing the Church in Poland was the persuasive influence of visions of the human person that denied the human capacity for free will. For the Marxists, human beings were products of their class and driven by economic interests. In the words of the Bolshevik theoretician Nikolai Bukharin, the individual human being is "filled with the influences of his environment, as the skin of a sausage is filled with sausage meat."[15] After the Second World War, Wojtyła and the Dominican scholar M. Albert Krąpiec set about developing a philosophical anthropology that would defend the dignity of the human person by focusing on the human capacity to rise above all manner of social, economic, and psychological conditioning through the exercise of a free will. This anthropology took its final academic form in the publication of his work *The Acting Person* in

---

[14] Adam Michnik, "After the Revolution, The New Dangers to the New Democracies," *The New Republic*, July 2, 1990, 28–29.

[15] Nikolai Bukharin, *Historical Materialism: A System of Sociology* (London/New York: Routledge, 2011), 98.

1969.[16] One of the most famous axioms presented in this work is that "action reveals the person." Having been influenced by currents in mid-twentieth century personalism and phenomenology, Wojtyła was interested in the relationship between truth, freedom, and human authenticity, and he set out to offer a sustained intellectual analysis of the inadequacies of the Marxist treatment of these themes. He was particularly critical of two types of inauthenticity he believed fostered the success of totalitarian ideologies in the twentieth century. These are similar to the Sartrean notion of bad faith. The first he described as servile conformism, the second as non-involvement.

Wojtyła acknowledged that the term "conformism" denotes a tendency to comply with the accepted custom and to resemble others, a tendency that in itself is neutral and in many further respects positive and constructive or even creative, and indeed, this constructive and creative assimilation in the community is a confirmation and also a manifestation of human solidarity. Nonetheless, he also observed that, when this normal and healthy social tendency to "fit in" begins to sway towards servility, it becomes highly negative.[17] Conformism "consists primarily in an attitude of compliance or resignation, in a specific form of passivity that makes the person to be but the subject of what happens instead of being the actor or agent responsible for building his own attitudes and his own commitment to the community."[18] The servile conformist "fails to accept his share in constructing the community and allows himself to be carried with and by the anonymous majority."[19] Inauthenticity, which takes the form of a servile conformism, equals "a weakness of personal transcendence and a weakness of the capacity for self-determination and of choice."[20]

This pathology was well illustrated by Eugène Ionescu in his play *The Rhinoceros*, written in 1959. The play belongs to the school of drama known as the Theatre of the Absurd. Over the course of three acts, all except one of the inhabitants of a provincial French town believe that they are a rhinoceros and behave accordingly. At first the majority regard those who are walking about on all four limbs and trying to make the sounds of a rhinoceros a joke, but by the third act almost the entire town is behaving in this manner, because this is what other people are doing.

While Ionescu's play made fun of the totalitarian mentality by imag-

---

[16] Karol Wojtyła, *The Acting Person* (Boston: D. Reidel, 1979).

[17] Ibid., 289.

[18] Ibid.

[19] Ibid.

[20] Ibid., 346.

ining a village in which people think of themselves as rhinos just because this is what other people are doing, a similar artistic device was employed throughout the 1980s by the leaders of the Orange Alternative Movement.[21] Their aim was also to point out the absurdity of the totalitarian mentality through recourse to comedy. The movement started in Wroclaw and was led by Waldemar Fydrych, commonly known as the Major. On June 1, 1988, in an event known as the revolution of dwarves, more than ten thousand persons marched through the centre of Wroclaw wearing orange dwarf hats. The police were aware that if they asked the participants the question "Why did you participate in an illegal meeting of dwarfs?" they would look utterly ridiculous. The Orange Alternative movement had its intellectual origins in Dadaism and surrealism, but in a politically powerful way, it illustrated Wojtyła's more densely philosophical criticisms of the capacity of "servile conformism" to undermine human freedom and dignity.

The second form of inauthenticity identified by Wojtyła—that of "non-involvement"—is defined as a stoic egocentrism according to which the person deliberately withdraws from making decisions and taking social actions. Whereas servile conformists tend not to question or judge, those who take a stance of non-involvement are fully conscious of the wrong that is being done, but they lack the courage to intervene on the side of those being oppressed. Much of what happened in the mid-twentieth century could have been avoided if these two forms of inauthenticity were not common dispositions.

How did these social pathologies arise? Wojtyła argued that, in a sense, they have always been around since the time when things went wrong in the Garden of Eden. However, he believed that the intellectual history of post-eighteenth-century Europe fostered the tendencies by promoting a false notion of freedom. In a speech he delivered to the scholars of Lublin University (KUL) in 1987, he expressed the idea in the following terms: "The human person must in the name of the truth about himself stave off a double temptation: the temptation to make the truth about himself subordinate to his freedom and the temptation to make himself subordinate to the world of objects; he has to refuse to succumb to the temptation of both self-idolatry and of self-subjectification: *Positus est in medio homo: nec bestia—nec deus.*"[22]

---

[21] See Juliusz Tyszka, "The Orange Alternative: Street Happenings as Social Performance in Poland under Martial Law," *New Theatre Quarterly* 14, no. 56 (1998): 311–23.

[22] Karol Wojtyła, "Address to the Scholars at the Catholic University of Lublin," *Christian Life in Poland* (November 1987), 51.

In his 1985 essay "Communism as a Cultural Foundation," Leszek Kołakowski offered a similar reading to that of Wojtyła. Communism, he said, emerged from the tradition of the Enlightenment, and in conditions where traditional beliefs had been abandoned by educated elites, it took the form of a secular religion. However, he observed that as a religion it suffered from an internal dialectic. It simultaneously demanded both blind obedience or faith and acceptance of it as a rational interpretation of the world. According to Kołakowski, "communism's hovering between the two irreconcilable concepts led in time to a collapse within its empire of both rationalism and religion; and its ideological bankruptcy was at the same time a defeat for the Enlightenment, of which it was the ultimate, most consistent, and thus most self-destructive expression."[23] This general critique was expressed somewhat more poetically by Professor Krasnodębski, who said that Marxism was not an exotic venereal disease brought into Europe by those whose natural habitat may be found in the seedier quarters of Asia: it resulted not from the betrayal of the values of modern (Enlightenment) humanism, but rather from the radical and consequential realization of them.[24]

These various contradictions within the political culture of the West led Wojtyła to argue that the Western world is currently at a cross roads between what he termed "a culture of death" that acknowledges no absolute truth or goodness, and for which, in such circumstances, power is the only legitimate political currency, and a civilization of love built upon notions of the sanctity of human life and culture-transcendent truth and goodness. In poetic form he expressed the price of this choice in the following words:

Freedom—a continuing conquest
It cannot simply be possessed!
It comes as a gift, but keeping it is a struggle
Gift and struggle are inscribed on pages, hidden yet open.
For freedom you pay with all your being, therefore call that your
    freedom
Which allows you, in paying the price,
To possess yourself anew.
At such a price do we enter history and touch her epochs.

---

[23] Leszek Kołakowski, "Communism as a Cultural Formation," *Survey* 29, no .2 (Summer 1985): 147.
[24] Krasnodębski, "W oczekiwaniu na supermarkety," 73.

Where is the dividing-line between those generations who paid
    too little
And those who paid too much?
On which side of that line are we?[25]

In 1979, in the first year of his pontificate, Wojtyła returned to Poland for a nine-day visit. This visit had a dramatic impact upon Polish
morale. His message, at its most simple, was "Be Not Afraid." The US National Security Advisor at the time, Zbigniew Brzezinski, was later to say
that the Polish people "all of a sudden discovered that they all shared the
same aspiration and the same resentments, and the regime discovered that
it was weak and isolated."[26] In an interview given at the time of Wojtyła's
death, Brzezinski explained Wojtyła's strength in the following terms:
"He grew up as a young adolescent under the Nazi occupation. Then he
lived under Stalinism. I think that taught him what happens when violence is institutionalized and tramples the human being. And then that
became deepened with a philosophy, a theology in which he really placed
fundamental and central emphasis on the sanctity of the human being and
on the mysterious divinity within each human being."[27]

Throughout the 1980s, the treatment of such themes as freedom,
courage, human authenticity, and human dignity in Wojtyła's literary and
philosophical works was popularized by the chaplains of Solidarity, foremost among whom were the philosopher Jozef Tischner, author of *The
Spirit of Solidarity*, and Jerzy Popiełuszko, whose speeches were broadcast-
ed over Radio Free Europe.[28] The following passage was typical of Popiełuszko's eloquence and his faith in what Havel called "the power of the
powerless": "Do not struggle with violence. Violence is a sign of weakness.
All those who cannot win through the heart try to conquer through violence. The most wonderful and durable struggles in history have been carried on by human thought. The most ignoble fights and most ephemeral
successes are those of violence. An idea which needs rifles to survive dies
of its own accord. An idea which is imposed by violence collapses under it.

---

[25] Karol Wojtyła, "Thinking my country," in *Memory and Identity: Personal Reflections*
    (London: Weidenfeld and Nicolson, 2005), 84.

[26] Margaret Warner, "A Discussion of the Legacy of Pope John Paul II featuring Zbigniew
    Brzezinski," *National Institute for the Renewal of the Priesthood*, April 7, 2005, accessed
    March 13, 2017, http://www.jknirp.com/zbig.htm.

[27] Ibid.

[28] Jozef Tischner, *The Spirit of Solidarity* (San Francisco: Harper and Row, 1984).

An idea capable of life wins without effort and is then followed by millions of people."[29]

The Polish intelligentsia (including Wojtyła) offered an intellectual critique of the social pathology that was really existing Communism and united with the workers through the agencies of KOR and Solidarity. Under the patronage of the Catholic Church led by Wojtyła, it was able to change perceptions of what was politically possible and desirable. Communism as a twentieth-century form of the applications of the principles of Machiavelli was ultimately defeated by a set of contrary principles that included the notions of the power of the powerless, living in truth, and solidarity between the social classes.

Poles as a national group have a reputation for being romantics, for putting principles above pragmatics. In many moments of history, this does not seem to have helped them, but in the summer of 1989, truth and courage and romantic ideals triumphed over lies and thuggery. A coalition of intellectuals, workers, students, and the Catholic hierarchy asserted sufficient moral and professional authority for the Communists to have no choice but to peacefully surrender their power to a new generation of Polish leaders. This particular chapter in Polish history has become for students of political theory the model of how to transform a totalitarian society without recourse to violence. It is also a model of how to contend with the culture of death.

---

[29] Jerzy Popiełusko, as cited in Robert Royal, "Fr. Popielusko and Communist Poland," *Arlington Catholic Herald* (2000), accessed March 13, 2017, http://www.catholiceduca-tion.org/en/controversy/persecution/fr-popielusko-and-communist-poland.html. See also Robert Royal, *The Catholic Martyrs of the Twentieth Century* (New York: Cross-road, 2000).

CHAPTER 8

Natural Law: From Neo-Thomism to Nuptial Mysticism[1]

FERGUS KERR SUBTITLED a recent survey of twentieth-century theological trends "From neo-scholasticism to nuptial mysticism."[2] While this subtitle may stand as a one sentence summary of the sweep of twentieth-century Catholic theological tendencies, a similar trajectory can be observed at work in the more microlevel territory of natural law doctrine. For decades now, natural law has been presented to Catholic undergraduates as a kind of *lingua franca* for dialogue with nonbelievers precisely because it was deemed possible to sever it from its theological roots. This is notwithstanding the fact that Protestants have never really been all that keen on it, regarding it as something of Stoic rather than biblical provenance, and notwithstanding the further facts that it depends on a conception of nature as something stable and that this has been rejected by most contemporary postmoderns.

When one eliminates Protestants and postmoderns, those left standing are usually liberals. It is largely in order to find a common language with them that attempts have been made to formulate a version of natural law that does not rely on any particular theological framework. However, leaving aside all the theoretical objections that have been raised against

---

[1] First Published in *Communio: International Catholic Review* 35 (Fall 2008): 374–96.

[2] Fergus Kerr, *Twentieth Century Catholic Theologians: From Neo-Scholasticism to Nuptial Mysticism* (Oxford: Blackwell, 2007). The terms "neo-Scholasticism" and "neo-Thomism" are often used interchangeably, though the former is a little broader, encompassing the whole range of the modern retrieval of medieval thought, especially the retrieval that took place prior to the Second Vatican Council. In this article the work of Jacques Maritain will be treated as the flagship of neo-Thomism.

this project, the sociological fact is that it has not been a strategic success. Liberals just don't buy the medicine, even when the theological ingredients have been expressly excluded and the principles have been repackaged in explicitly liberal idioms.[3] This often leads to a situation in which Catholics talk to other Catholics in an idiom that was devised for dialogue with unbelievers, while the unbelievers are either not persuaded or so poorly educated as to be unfamiliar with the idiom. When natural law is marketed as universally reasonable without any accompanying theological baggage, it can begin to sound, in Russell Hittinger's memorable phrase, like "a doctrine for Cartesian minds somehow under Church discipline."[4]

It was perhaps for such reasons that Cardinal Ratzinger, as he was, described natural law as a "blunt instrument" in dialogues with secular society.[5] This was not because he personally rejected belief in natural law, but because he believed that it presupposes a concept of nature in which nature and reason overlap, a view that he further claimed was "capsized" with the arrival of the theory of evolution.[6] Without a foundational belief in a divinely created cosmos, the doctrine falls on incredulous ears. It lacks persuasive force. Postmoderns will never buy it because they have rejected a notion of nature that includes stable essences, and liberals never buy it because individual autonomy occupies such a high place in their hierarchy of goods that it trumps appeals to any notion of there being one single vision of a "good life." For John Rawls, arguably the most influential liberal theorist of the twentieth century, if people want to devote their lives to counting blades of grass, then that is the good for them.[7] Reason has been truncated to finding efficient ways of achieving ends, and nature is now subject to scientific manipulation, so neither reason nor nature are strong foundations upon which to build bridges to the contemporary liberal tradition.

Nonetheless, Catholic apologists for several decades have been attempting to defend a Catholic view of the good life in the forums of liberal society using the vocabulary of natural law. Many have done so in an al-

---

[3] For a partial analysis of this lack of strategic success see K. Lee, "Contemporary Challenges to Natural Law Theories," *The Catholic Social Science Review* 12 (2007): 41–50.

[4] Russell Hittinger, *First Grace: Rediscovering the Natural Law in a Post-Christian World* (Wilmington, DE: ISI Books, 2003), 62.

[5] Joseph Ratzinger, *Values in a Time of Upheaval* (San Francisco: Ignatius Press, 2006), 38–39.

[6] Joseph Ratzinger and Jürgen Habermas, *Dialectics of Secularization: On Reason and Religion* (San Francisco: Ignatius Press, 2006), 69–70.

[7] John A. Rawls, *Theory of Justice* (Cambridge, MA: Harvard University Press, 1999), 379.

most axiomatic belief that it is a *lingua franca* for dialogue with nonbelievers. They have been told that this was recognized at the Nuremburg trials and that it was a project promoted by the French Thomist and advisor of Paul VI Jacques Maritain, who contributed to the drafting of the United Nations' *Universal Declaration on Human Rights* (1948), which itself is upheld as the project's greatest achievement, or at least an example of what can be achieved.

Between 1948 and the first decade of the twenty-first century, however, Western society underwent a cultural revolution. When Maritain was at the height of his academic career in the 1940s, there were no contraceptive pills, no IVF babies, no embryo experimentations, no clonings, no internet, and no space satellites, to name but a few of the socially significant new factors. Christianity, though divided and battered on every side by Freudians, Marxists, and atheistic existentialists, was still providing something of a moral compass for the majority of people who lived and worked outside of intellectual and artistic circles. By 1968, however, in Maritain's twilight years, the various alternative visions of what a human being is— and hence, what the meaning of life is—had captured the imaginations of the postwar generation, and with the expansion of higher education to the lower middle and working classes, an entire anti-Christian cultural revolution was effected. The preferred cocktail of the generation of '68 contained ingredients from Freud (sexuality needs to be liberated from religious constraints), Marx (economics is the major factor determining life's choices), and Nietzsche (the meaning of life is discovered in the quest for individuality and originality of lifestyle), and it was widely bought by people outside the artistic fringe or the intellectual avant-garde and then taken into suburbia.

Meanwhile, within the great universities, the Enlightenment project of formulating a universally acceptable ethical framework with recourse to reason alone was of dwindling interest. The project was kept alive in some philosophy and social science departments of British and American universities, particularly in places proud of their eighteenth-century philosophers, like Cambridge and Edinburgh, but nonetheless, the ascendant view was that the quest for universal reason was oppressive—indeed, it was even maligned as a factor contributing to two world wars—and the romantic values of originality and individuality and the concomitant interest in traditions and cultures had taken its place. While Marx's ideal man was to hunt in the morning, fish in the afternoon, and rear cattle in the evening, the ideal postmodern could be heterosexual in the morning, homosexual after lunch, and bisexual in the evening. In other words, the postmoderns tended to be against both reason (understood in anything other than an instrumental sense) and nature (understood as a normative concept embodying stable essences). In such a culture (both intellectual and popular), it is hard to see how references to natural law could fulfill the function of a *lingua franca*.

By the 1990s, at least some Catholic scholars were beginning to question whether the Maritain project and its subsidiaries were still the most strategically viable options. Foremost among these Catholic scholars was Alasdair MacIntyre. As a former Marxist, MacIntyre often showed a more acute understanding of the Church's intellectual enemies than did cradle Catholics educated at elite Catholic institutions. He wrote perceptively about the liberal tradition's employment of ideological idioms to paper-over or mask contentious theological fault lines, and he was critical of the Kantian turn in Thomism.[8] His reservations have been acknowledged in various ways by John Haldane, James V. Schall, Robert P. Kraynak, Thaddeus Kozinski, Graham McAleer, and a raft of other names among the youngest generation of Catholic scholars. In *Faithful Reason: Essays Catholic and Philosophical*, Haldane observed that "anyone reviewing the degree of ideological and moral diversity exhibited today, half a century after Maritain wrote *The Person and the Common Good*, must wonder how feasible is the project of a civil society and political culture based on natural law."[9] In *Jacques Maritain: The Philosopher in Society*, Schall noted that "the reason natural law assumes such importance for Maritain is because he takes it to be an objective and neutral way of talking about and understanding human activity on a philosophic basis that directly implies no revelational content."[10] This, however, raises the question of whether there is a theologically neutral account of nature, and it is this aspect of the project that has been receiving the most extensive criticism over the past decade. It should be noted that this essay is not a statement against the idea of natural law per se, but a recognition that the Maritain project no longer appears viable or, in other words, that natural law is no longer, if it ever was, a *lingua franca* between Catholics and liberals.

Even earlier, in 1969, in his extensive commentary on the notion of human dignity in *Gaudium et Spes*, Cardinal Ratzinger described as nothing

---

[8] Alasdair MacIntyre, *Three Rival Versions of Moral Enquiry* (London: Duckworth, 1990).

[9] John Haldane, *Faithful Reason: Essays Catholic and Philosophical* (London: Routledge, 2004), 150.

[10] James Schall, *Jacques Maritain: The Philosopher in Society* (Oxford: Rowman and Littlefield, 1998), 88.

more than a "fiction" the notion that it is "possible to construct a rational philosophical picture of man intelligible to all and on which all men of goodwill can agree, the actual Christian doctrines being added to this as a sort of crowning conclusion."[11] While such criticisms sounded like an off-key performance at that time, much contemporary natural-law thinking actually begins with the anthropological foundations set down in §22 of *Gaudium et Spes*, the explicitly Christocentric section preferred by Wojtyła and Ratzinger, which renders the Christian doctrine foundational, rather than a "crowning conclusion." For Ratzinger and many contemporary Catholic moral theologians, natural law presupposes a Trinitarian Creator God. The idea that a theologically neutral or a merely theistically colored account of human nature and its dignity could provide an adequate foundation for its defense is being explicitly rejected.[12] Cardinal Angelo Scola has argued that a culture that does not accept the revelation of the Trinitarian God ultimately renders itself incapable of understanding sexual difference in a positive sense.[13] In other words, the Church cannot ultimately defend her teaching on such subjects as marriage and the reservation of the priesthood to those of the male sex without recourse to Trinitarian anthropology. This need not mean, of course, that reason can tell us nothing about human nature; it means, rather, that what reason can tell us is intrinsically open to and finds its fulfillment in the revelation of the triune God. The problem is not the idea of a stable, God-created nature; the problem is the de-theologizing construal of that stability as neutral to the Creator.

In his 1990 essay "Grace and the Form of Nature and Culture," David L. Schindler concluded that "there is and can be—in the concrete historical order which is ours—no nature or natural laws which are neutral in religious form" and, consequently, that "the common ground for which the Christian seeks in his natural law argument, is and can only be within the concrete history of the dialogue partners."[14] In other words, the theological baggage that had been thrown overboard should be brought back

---

11 Joseph Ratzinger, "The Dignity of the Human Person," in *Commentary on the Documents of Vatican II*, vol. 5, ed. H. Vorgrimler (New York: Herder and Herder, 1969), 119.

12 Walter Kasper, "The Theological Anthropology of *Gaudium et Spes*," *Communio* 23 (Spring 1996): 129–41; David L. Schindler, "Christology and the *Imago Dei*: Interpreting *Gaudium et Spes*," *Communio* 23 (Spring 1996): 156–84.

13 Angelo Scola, "The Dignity and Mission of Women: The Anthropological and Theological Foundations," *Communio* 25 (Spring 1998): 42–56, at 52.

14 David L. Schindler, "Grace and the Form of Nature and Culture" in *Catholicism and Secularization in America*, ed. David L. Schindler (Huntington, IN: Communio Books, 1990), 23–24.

into dialogues with non-Catholic parties. Rather than being dressed up as something fashionably liberal, which will repel evangelical Protestants and almost all postmoderns and convince no liberals into the bargain, natural law is now more often presented in the context of an explicitly Trinitarian and largely Christocentric anthropology and the moral theology that flows from it. The new theological idiom enveloping both is that of nuptial mysticism that has received its most extensive treatment in the works of John Paul II, Cardinal Scola, and Cardinal Marc Ouellet.[15] It has as its foundation the theological anthropology of *Gaudium et Spes* §22, which includes within it the notion of an epithalamic relationship between Christ and the human person. This will not make it any more palatable to liberals, but it may mean that members of the Catholic laity who are not professional philosophers and theologians will be presented with a much more theologically enriched account of what the Church means by natural law in the many magisterial documents in which it appears. It may clear up the confusion while Catholic scholars put more energy into unmasking the metaphysical presuppositions of the liberal tradition, bringing into sharper relief the relentlessly profane, and some would argue androgynous, account of human dignity that pervades liberal theory.[16]

Such an approach may be found in Eberhard Schockenhoff's *Natural Law and Human Dignity: Universal Ethics in an Historical World*. Schockenhoff suggested that the life of the Christian churches must "bear witness to the inherent rationality of the high ethical teachings contained in the biblical history of revelation" and present them in an "open contest about the *humanum*, where the various world religions, political utopias, and secular humanisms challenge each other."[17] In such a contest, it becomes your god against our God, your vision of human dignity against our vision. The intellectual shadowboxing is over and the practical consequences of the acceptance of different theological starting points can be pushed to the center of the debate. As Ratzinger wrote in an essay on interreligious dialogue, "the point of this dialogue was not simply to repeat

---

[15] Angelo Scola, *The Nuptial Mystery* (Grand Rapids, MI: Eerdmans, 2005); Marc Ouellet, *Divine Likeness: Toward a Trinitarian Anthropology of the Family* (Grand Rapids, MI: Eerdmans, 2006).

[16] For an account of liberal metaphysics as fundamentally androgynous and gay, see David S. Crawford, "Liberal Androgyny: 'Gay Marriage' and the Meaning of Sexuality in our Time," *Communio* 33 (Summer 2006): 239–65.

[17] Eberhard Schockenhoff, *Natural Law and Human Dignity: Universal Ethics in an Historical World*, trans. Brian McNeil (Washington, DC: Catholic University of America Press, 2003), 284.

nineteenth and early twentieth century scholarship in comparative religion, which, from the lofty height of a liberal-rationalistic standpoint, had judged the religions with the self-assurance of enlightened reason."[18] Since there is now a "broad consensus that such a standpoint is an impossibility," (that is, a broad consensus that we need to move beyond Kant), in order to understand religion, "it is necessary to experience it from within, and indeed ... only such experience, which is inevitably particular and tied to a definite historical starting-point, can lead the way to mutual understanding."[19] Enlightened reason, as he says, has a wax nose! What follows offers a survey of recent scholarship on natural law from this or closely-related strategic perspectives.

Matthew Levering began his *Biblical Natural Law* with the observation that "natural law doctrine does not become significantly more persuasive or effective once pluralism dictates the exclusion of biblical revelation."[20] He believes that "no matter how nuanced the schemes for exhibiting basic requirements of human flourishing or however much one attempts to provide an autonomous role for human practical reason apart from natural teleologies" implanted by the Creator, there are insuperable difficulties: "the 'human flourishing' answers reduce to sophisticated pragmatism rather than real 'law'; the 'practical reason' answers appear to be a premature restriction of the possibilities of human freedom in ever-evolving history."[21] Accordingly, the focus of his *Biblical Natural Law* is on exploring three questions: whether there are biblical warrants for natural law doctrine, what kind of natural law doctrine biblical texts support, and what happens when natural law doctrine is left out of constructive ethics arising from the Bible.

Levering proposes four constructive principles, centered upon biblical texts, for understanding the relationship between Christian ethics, biblical revelation, and natural law doctrine:

[First] Scripture presents certain goods as constitutive of true human flourishing and thus of moral order. *Genesis* 1–2 provides one place where such teleological ordering, rooted theocentrically in God's creative providence, can be seen. Here we find in germ

---

[18] Joseph Ratzinger, "Interreligious Dialogue and Jewish-Christian Relations," *Communio* 25 (Spring 1998): 29–40, at 31.

[19] Ibid.

[20] Matthew Levering, *Biblical Natural Law* (Oxford: Oxford University Press, 2008), 18.

[21] Ibid., 17. Levering is coeditor of *Nova et Vetera* (English).

the human natural inclinations. . . . God creates human beings so that they are naturally ordered to preserve the good of their human existence. Without the inclination to preserve this good, God's warning about the tree of the knowledge of good and evil would not be intelligible. . . . God also inscribes within human beings an inclination toward the good of procreation and toward knowing the truth, ultimately the truth about the Creator.[22]

[Second] Scripture does not countenance an absolute disjunction between divine positive law and natural law. . . . God in giving the Decalogue connects obedience to the Decalogue with a glorious new creation in justice—a renewed creation that reverses the Fall. . . . Jesus retains the Decalogue in the form given to Israel.[23]

[Third] The Bible's understanding of law is theocentric. Law does not first pertain to "nature" or to human "reason." . . . Law has its ground in God, not in human beings. Our participated wisdom cannot be understood without adverting to its divine source. We do not constitute wisdom, but rather we receive it by seeking to discern and participate in it.[24]

[Fourth] The grace of the Holy Spirit does not negate, but rather fulfils the law's precepts.[25]

Given these four premises, "the question cannot be whether Christian ethics must import an extrinsic system of natural law," but rather, "Christian moral theology requires a philosophically sophisticated natural law doctrine in order to do justice to the teachings of divine revelation."[26] This is because "ultimately the work of Christ and the Holy Spirit fulfils the natural law in us and elevates us to Communion with the Trinity."[27]

This last principle sits well with the classically Thomist definition of natural law as a participation of the rational creature in the eternal law, a doctrine that opens natural law, in turn, to theological anthropology

---

[22] Ibid., 59–60.

[23] Ibid., 61–62.

[24] Ibid., 63–65. In this context, Levering makes reference to material in the books of Wisdom, Sirach, and Proverbs.

[25] Ibid., 65.

[26] Ibid., 67.

[27] Ibid., 176.

and nuptial mysticism. The link between the two is the notion of life as a "theo-drama." In Balthasar's terms, the natural law is perfected and fulfilled by the ecstatic movement of a person's response to Christ's love and, hence, participation in the life of the Trinity.

This placement of natural law within a theo-dramatic and explicitly Trinitarian context helps to overcome the moralism or, to use Ratzinger's more specific term, "Pious Pelagianism" that had been fostered by the tendency to sever the study of spirituality from moral theology and a purely philosophical account of natural law from revelation.[28] There might be, in other words, a united Thomist-Balthasarian front on an account of natural law rooted in Trinitarian anthropology, but this does entail a critique of elements of neo-Thomism.[29]

Arguably, the twentieth-century Thomist who came closest to offering a moral theology with an accent on theo-dramatics was the Belgian Dominican Servais-Théodore Pinckaers.[30] Against the neo-Thomist tendency to mute the theological dimensions of the doctrine of natural law, Pinckaers emphasized that Catholic ethics transforms Aristotle, since "the advent of divine revelation has occasioned a profound transformation in the doctrine of virtue according to which the first source of moral excellence is . . . located in . . . God through Christ."[31] He noted that this transformation is evident in the doctrine of the infused moral virtues, which are not acquired by unaided human effort, but are implanted in the human person by the Holy Spirit. Accordingly, "in moral theology, the point is not to observe the commandments of the Decalogue materially, to obey them so as to fulfill one's obligations or through a sense of duty; the

---

[28] Lorenzo Albacete has described moralism as a modern form of Pelagianism, a belief in salvation through good works and obedience, which he suggests can be overcome only by a "proper theology of grace in which grace is not presented as something added to and external to the natural law itself, but rather as the possibility of a personal encounter with Jesus Christ" ("The Pope against Moralism and Legalism," *Anthropotes* 10 [1994]: 85).

[29] In this context, for instance, Schockenhoff has emphasized the importance of the distinction between the passive participation of irrational creatures in the divine reason that governs the world and the actively regulating participation on the part of the human person, and he has also acknowledged that this distinction was often "flattened" in presentations about the natural law by neo-Thomists (*Natural Law and Human Dignity*, 159).

[30] Pinckaers was raised in a Walloon region of Belgium by a Dutch-speaking father and a Walloon mother and was, from 1983 until his death in 2008, based at the Albertinum at the University of Fribourg in Switzerland.

[31] Servais-Théodore Pinckaers, *Morality: A Catholic View* (South Bend, IN: St. Augustine's Press, 2001), 71. Of course, one must add that there is a case to be made that Aristotle, too, connects ethics and the divine, since, even for Aristotle, nature depends on God.

point is to observe them out of love, with the heart."[32] Pinckaers believed that the lack of attention to the Sermon on the Mount in much of twentieth-century Catholic moral thought can be explained by the fact that it is not easily integrated into a systematization of moral theology based on obligations. Whereas moral systems of obligation are by nature static, the teaching of the Sermon on the Mount is fundamentally dynamic: "it is animated by a continuous tendency toward exceeding and surpassing, a tendency toward the progress and perfection of love in imitation of the Father's goodness."[33] Moreover, for Pinckaers, "there is no real separation between the moral part of the *Summa* and its two dogmatic parts: the doctrine on the Trinity, in particular on the Word and on the Holy Spirit, found in the *prima pars*, pertains to the morality set forth in the *secunda pars* that we can thus identify as Trinitarian and spiritual."[34] He further claims that, in a parallel way, the doctrine of the *tertia pars* on Christ and the mystical Body is intimately linked to Aquinas's moral teaching, which is Christological and ecclesial.[35] Pinckaers's fundamentally Trinitarian framework for moral theology and the treatment of natural law within it thus provides an alternative from within the Dominican tradition to various currents of neo-Thomism.

In his *Aquinas, Ethics, and Philosophy of Religion: Metaphysics and Practice*,[36] Thomas Hibbs takes things in a similar direction. He observes that the contemporary interest in the Trinity, in creation, in the bestowal of the gift of being, and in the primacy of the virtue of charity is transforming our understanding of how metaphysics is related to practice.[37] In particular, he believes that the ultimate foundation for Aquinas's account of natural law is precisely his understanding of the internal life of God as self-communicative love, even if the Trinitarian accent is not strong in his direct references to natural law.[38] He suggests that, once one asks the question of

---

[32] Servais-Théodore Pinckaers, *The Pinckaers Reader: Renewing Thomistic Moral Theology*, ed. J. Berkman and C. S. Titus (Washington, DC: Catholic University of America Press, 2005), 52.

[33] Ibid.

[34] Ibid., 28.

[35] Ibid., 29.

[36] Thomas Hibbs, *Aquinas, Ethics, and the Philosophy of Religion: Metaphysics and Practice* (Bloomington, IN: Indiana University Press, 2007), 102. See also Hibbs, "Divine Irony and Natural Law: Speculation and Edification in Aquinas," *International Philosophical Quarterly* 30 (1990): 426.

[37] Hibbs, *Aquinas, Ethics, and the Philosophy of Religion*, xiii.

[38] Hibbs laments the eclipse of the more Platonic and Dionysian dimensions of Thomist metaphysics in neo-Thomism. Indeed, he argues that "misconceptions of the nature

how the eternal law is promulgated and receives the response ("promulgation occurs through word and writing, through the Divine Word and the Book of Life"), one is into the territory of natural law and a metaphysics of participation.[39] The latter leads in turn to the issue of the way in which the conditions of the soul make it more or less receptive to discerning the principles of the natural law. Here Hibbs argues that, "even where there is the possibility of derivation of human laws from the natural law, Aquinas does not advocate anything like the abstract, context-free model of practical reasoning found in twentieth-century decision-making models."[40] Rather, "for Aquinas, the inherent deficiencies in any deductive model of morality underscore the indispensable role for prudence even in natural law."[41]

The recovery of prudence that is currently under way signals another area in which the classical natural law tradition can be integrated into the notion of theo-drama. Prudence, after all, is good moral sense, which one exercises in light of the overall narrative thrust of one's life-story—that is, in light of one's role in the theo-drama.

St. Thomas identified no fewer than eight quasi-integral parts of prudence: memory, understanding, docility, ingeniousness, reason, foresight, circumspection, and caution. Pamela Hall argues that this catalogue shows that for the making of a prudential judgment, Aquinas required not merely deliberative skills but also an experience-gathering ability, and Kenneth L. Schmitz has drawn attention to the fact that not all experience is of the same wisdom-inducing quality.[42] Some experiences are sapiential, while others can be destructive of the soul's capacity to recognize the beautiful, the true, and the good and to be attracted to them. Education (or what the German Romantics called *Bildung*) and prudential judg-

---

of metaphysical enquiry have infected certain strains of Thomism for many centuries" and, in particular, that "there has been an eclipse of the erotic appeal of metaphysics and its pervasive deployment of aesthetic language." These misconceptions omit Aquinas's notion of "reason as participant in an order that encompasses it and exceeds its grasp, the prominent role of erotic and aesthetic discourse throughout his metaphysics; the intimate connection, in his theology, between the Trinity as exemplar of human action and the development of a social ontology of individuals-in-relation, and the construal of ethics itself as a mimetic practice" (ibid., 2).

[39] Ibid., 34.

[40] Ibid., 21.

[41] Ibid.

[42] Pamela Hall, *Narrative and the Natural Law: An Interpretation of Thomistic Ethics* (Notre Dame, IN: University of Notre Dame Press, 1994), 40; and Kenneth L. Schmitz, "St. Thomas and the Appeal to Experience," *Catholic Theological Society of America Proceedings* 47 (1992): 1–20.

ment are interconnected. As Pinckaers expressed the idea, the "work of prudence is not limited to determining what is permitted or forbidden but searches for excellence, a certain perfection of action in the existing situation, it requires the involvement of all the subject's faculties and the use of the external abilities acquired, among other things, by education."[43] The whole category of human experience and its significance for discerning the principles of the natural law is thus beginning to attract the attention of Catholic scholars who differ from those associated with the nihilist wing of the romantic tradition in emphasizing that not all experiences are potentially sapiential.

Robert Sokolowski's essay "What Is Natural Law? Human Purposes and Natural Ends" has been a leading contribution in this context and has been described as an attempt to "shed light on how natural law is promulgated in human experience."[44] With reference to the famous statement of St. Paul in his *Letter to the Romans* regarding the law written on the hearts of the Gentiles (Rom 2:14–15), Sokolowski writes that we should understand the full meaning of the words used for the heart (*cor* and *kardia*) in such passages: "they do not connote the separation of heart and head that we take for granted in a world shaped by Descartes."[45] He endorses Robert Spaemann's claim that, in the New Testament, the heart is taken to be a deeper recipient of truth than even the mind or intellect in Greek philosophy; it deals, rather, with the person's willingness to accept the truth.[46] Kevin O'Reilly makes a similar point in his essay "The Vision of Virtue and Knowledge of the Natural Law in Thomas Aquinas,"[47] in which he

---

[43] Pinckaers, *Reader*, 70.

[44] Robert Sokolowski, "What Is Natural Law? Human Purposes and Natural Ends," *The Thomist* 68 (2004): 507–29, at 526, repr. in Sokolowski, *Christian Faith and Human Understanding* (Washington, DC: Catholic University of America Press, 2006), 214–37.

[45] Sokolowski, *Christian Faith and Human Understanding*, 230. Michael Downey has also argued that for many of the medieval scholastics, including St. Bernard of Clairvaux, William of St. Thierry, Aelred of Rievaulx, and St. Bonaventure, there was a notion of the heart as the locus of personal life and union with God through love, and importantly, the work of the heart was not separated from reason or *intellectus* ("Jean Vanier: Recovering the Heart," *Spirituality Today* 38 [Winter 1986]: 337–48). See also Dietrich von Hildebrand, *The Heart: An Analysis of Human and Divine Affectivity* (South Bend, IN: St. Augustine's Press, 2007).

[46] Sokolowski, "What Is Natural Law: Human Purposes and Natural Ends," 525. He recommends R. Spaemann, *Personen: Versuche über den Unterschied zwischen "Etwas" und "Jemand"* (Stuttgart: Klett-Cotta, 1996), 29–30.

[47] Kevin O'Reilly, "The Vision of Virtue and Knowledge of the Natural Law in Thomas Aquinas," *Nova et Vetera* (English) 5, no. 1 (2007):41–66.

acknowledges that, for St. Thomas, affectivity is integral to the perception of the human good, that "reason cannot escape the influences of social practices that furnish the context in which they necessarily operate," and that, accordingly, the virtue ethics and natural law theories presuppose the need for the other.[48]

MacIntyre's work is clearly seminal in this context. As early as *After Virtue*, he recognized that Kant had both a moral philosophy and a philosophy of psychology but did not relate them each to the other in a satisfactory way.[49] One result of this schism between ethics and psychology was the replacement of the concepts of virtue and character with those of choice and autonomy. The Kantian system of duties and universally applicable principles did not include within its order a place for relating dispositions of character to the principles of right action. Some neo-Thomist projects mirrored this kind of post-Kantian schism. MacIntyre's work seeks to overcome the schism and to explore the social conditions of knowledge and character development. Without giving way to ethical relativism, he does acknowledge the importance of culture and practices for moral development, and he is acutely sensitive to the ways in which values are tacitly mediated to plain persons through institutional practices. His conclusions converge with aspects of the thought of Michael Polanyi, especially Polanyi's account of the tacit acquisition of knowledge.[50]

In addition to MacIntyre's contribution, the earlier work on virtue by Josef Pieper is also seminal.[51] Along with the critiques of moralism presented in Balthasar's *Love Alone Is Credible*, Pieper's work was a significant formative influence on the moral theology of Joseph Ratzinger. By bringing together contemporary virtue ethics and natural law scholarship, the objective is to provide a vision of moral theology that is sufficiently multidimensional to include a place for affectivity, as well as the integral components of prudence (including the significance of memory, human experience, and education).

Thus, while the natural law is written on the hearts of the Gentiles, as St. Paul observed, the spiritual condition of their hearts, which ebbs and flows in response to the movements of grace and the experience of love and evil, can make the natural law more or less legible. This aware-

---

[48] Ibid., 60.

[49] Alasdair MacIntyre, *After Virtue* (London: Duckworth, 1981), 79.

[50] Michael Polanyi, *The Tacit Dimension* (Chicago: University of Chicago Press, 2009). This edition is a reprint of the 1966 work with a new foreword by Amartya Sen.

[51] Josef Pieper, *Four Cardinal Virtues* (Notre Dame, IN: University of Notre Dame Press, 1966); Pieper, *Faith, Hope, Love* (San Francisco: Ignatius Press, 1997).

ness is often lost in neo-Thomist accounts from which one derives the impression that the human mind is something like a computer into which one can plug an ethical hypothetical and receive the correct moral answer providing it deliberates upon a series of questions in a logical sequence. Such an approach that explicitly ignores the condition of the heart is in fact a very liberal-rationalist sort of approach, and it is not surprising, therefore, that Levering observes that it was precisely a rejection of the Thomist metaphysics of participation (which involves one's whole being) that has been the recurring motif in liberal theories of natural law.[52] In each of the eight versions of modern natural law he surveys, there is no possibility of any participation by a creature with its whole being within an eternal law.

The focus upon the mode of participation of the natural law within the eternal law and the significance of prudence and human experience is also leading to a renewal of interest in natural inclinations and their attraction to the good. Inasmuch as this renewal tends to highlight the ecstatic character of nature, it is another area in which traditional natural law thinking opens from within to incorporation in theo-drama.

At the end of *The Sources of Christian Ethics* (1995), Pinckaers devotes a chapter entirely to the natural inclinations and argues that our understanding of the natural inclinations has been profoundly distorted by nominalist polarities, especially the alleged opposition between freedom and nature. After Ockham, human nature and natural inclinations come to be seen as referring primarily to bodily inclinations, "impulses of the lower order, on the psychosomatic plane."[53] Levering concurs with

---

[52] His succinct summary of this genealogy deserves citing in full: "Absent the biblical Creator's teleological ordering, what then are the various options that modern natural law tries to provide? To judge by our overview of eight of the most influential modern philosophers, the answers take the following directions: to distinguish between mind and its bodily machine, the former imposing its own laws and the latter with no *telos* outside itself (Descartes, Kant); to constitute a commonwealth that by sheer power instantiates laws of nature which are expressions of the desire for self-preservation (Hobbes); to rely upon self-interested human emotions to preserve order (Hume and Hobbes); to turn the focus to individualistic preservation of one's property (Locke); to throw off the violent bonds of civilization and return to a state of nature governed by pity and minding one's own business (Rousseau); to affirm the law constituting role of each individual's practical reason (Kant) over against the threat of sub-human 'inclination' and 'nature'; to affirm the overcoming of all divisions by means of the necessary historical evolution of Spirit (Hegel); to master even history itself and freely reconstitute one's 'nature' at every moment (Nietzsche)" (Levering, *Biblical Natural Law*, 138–39).

[53] Pinckaers, *Sources of Christian Ethics*, 333.

Pinckaers and argues that one can see the beginnings of the modern split between anthropocentric and theocentric alternatives for articulating natural law doctrine in the divergence of Scotus from Aquinas.[54] In Levering's reading, Scotus attempted to displace human-to-human (distinguished from human-to-God relationships) from the ambit of the natural law and thereby opened the door to liberalism.[55] A similar argument has been advanced by Catherine Pickstock, who locates the decisive shift away from a metaphysics of participation in the work of Scotus, rendering Scotus, rather than Aquinas, the forerunner of the liberal tradition.[56]

Levering identifies the understanding of natural inclinations as a major fault line across contemporary schools of natural law scholarship. He suggests that the three most significant approaches are found in the works of Pinckaers, Martin Rhonheimer, and Graham McAleer and that, while Pinckaers and McAleer are capable of a higher synthesis, they are not compatible with Rhonheimer.[57] He notes that Rhonheimer's approach shares similarities to that of the "new natural law" theory proposed by John Finnis, Robert George, and Germain Grisez.[58] For Rhonheimer, natural law refers not to laws of nature known by speculative knowledge, but strictly to the judgments of practical reason about human acts. In Levering's reading of him, the crucial aspect is that an "order of nature" does not establish the moral pattern for human reason, but rather human reason "establishes,

---

[54] Matthew Levering, "God and Natural Law: Reflections on Genesis 22," *Modern Theology* 24, no. 2 (April 2008): 155.

[55] Ibid., 156.

[56] Catherine Pickstock, "Duns Scotus: His Historical and Contemporary Significance," *Modern Theology* 21, no. 4 (October 2005): 543–74.

[57] For example, Martin Rhonheimer, *Natural Law and Practical Reason: A Thomist View of Moral Autonomy* (New York: Fordham University Press, 2000); Rhonheimer, *Die Perspektive der Moral: Philosophische Grundlagen der Tugendethik* (Berlin: Akademie-Verlag, 2001); Rhonheimer, "Praktische Prinzipien, Naturgesetz und konkrete Handlungsurteile in tugendethischer Perspektive: Zur Diskussion über praktische Vernunft und 'lex naturalis' bei Thomas von Aquin," *Studia Moralia* 39 (2001): 113–58; Rhonheimer, "The Cognitive Structure of the Natural Law and the Truth of Subjectivity," *The Thomist* 67 (2003): 1–44; Rhonheimer, *The Perspective of the Acting Person: Essays in the Renewal of Thomistic Moral Philosophy* (Washington, DC: Catholic University of America, 2008); Graham McAleer, *Ecstatic Morality and Sexual Politics: A Catholic and Antitotalitarian Theory of the Body* (New York: Fordham University Press, 2005); Pinckaers, *Reader*, especially chapters 4 and 18.

[58] John Finnis, *Natural Law and Natural Rights* (Oxford: Clarendon, 1980); Finnis, *Aquinas* (Oxford: Oxford University Press, 1998); Robert. P. George, *In Defense of Natural Law* (Oxford: Oxford University Press, 2001).

formulates, or promulgates" its own moral pattern.[59] Levering raises the following critical questions about Rhonheimer's approach:

> First, does Rhonheimer's account of the *Imago Dei* as an image precisely in its constitutive power adequately appreciate the role of receptivity and contemplation in human rationality? Related to this question does he separate the "practical" from the "speculative" aspect of reason too firmly, out of concern that human reason norm non-rational nature, rather than human reason receiving a norm from non-rational nature? Second, does his view of a level of "pure naturalness" in the human body, for example what he calls a "mere attraction between bodies," properly understand the hylomorphic unity of the hierarchically ordered inclinations in the human person?[60]

Levering believes that it is precisely the neglect of the more erotic dimensions of Thomism, to which Hibbs has also drawn attention, that is responsible for the inadequacies in Rhonheimer's approach to the topic of human inclinations: "The work of humanization, for Rhonheimer, produces from the water of 'nature,' the wine of 'human nature.' But the water, as Pinckaers and McAleer show clearly, is already wine; the point of unity is the movement of *ecstasis* toward the good that belongs to the natural inclinations, a movement perfected by (not constituted by) the virtues. Their metaphysical work, following Aquinas, illumines the consistency of teleology; the attraction of the good in God's creative artistry."[61]

In contrast to Rhonheimer, Levering suggests that "Pinckaers engages the whole metaphysical fabric of natural law doctrine: the hylomorphic unity of the body and soul; the nature of the good, and perfection, happiness and friendship as constitutive of the doctrine of natural law and natural inclinations."[62] He further argues that Pinckaers's deeply Trinitarian foundations for the doctrine of natural law can be enriched by ideas presented in McAleer's *Ecstatic Morality and Sexual Politics*. In this work, McAleer attempts to develop a theology of the body on the basis of St. Thomas's analysis of matter (in the *Sentences*), theories of substantial composition and ecstatic being (from the *Summa contra gentiles*), and the understanding of concupiscence (found in the *Summa theologica*). In this

---

[59] Levering, *Biblical Natural Law*, 154.
[60] Ibid., 162–63.
[61] Ibid., 186.
[62] Ibid., 143.

context, the word "ecstatic" is a reference to the Thomistic insight that all the parts of creation (including the human body) are disposed towards service one for another and that the natural appetite seeks the divine likeness as its own perfection.[63]

McAleer's approach self-consciously builds on themes in John Paul II's theology of the body and the encyclical *Veritatis Splendor* (especially §§20, 21, and 24).[64] The influence of St. John of the Cross finds its imprint in the Wojtyłian account of natural law as founded on Christ and "interiorly structured by the exemplar of Christ's love on the Cross."[65] Natural law "establishes a dynamism in the body that calls the person to participation in the eternal law of God's wisdom and love."[66] Moreover, since it is Christological, McAleer observes that natural law cannot be understood apart from the spousal relationship of Christ with his Church.[67] In a project that is in many ways parallel to that of Hibbs, McAleer thus tries to present a more "erotic" Aquinas. To that end, he focuses upon the Thomistic treatment of the relationship between desire and its object, the relationship between matter and form. He notes that St. Thomas argued that matter and form are always already internally related: "Creatures are intrinsically structured to an other-directedness through which they yet attain their own proper power (*ST* I, q.19, a.2): they are thus internally ecstatic, a consequence of their being good and so interiorly propelled to communicating that good: *bonum est diffusivum sui.*"[68]

Paradoxically, McAleer's explicitly Christocentric treatment of moral theology, natural law, and the inclinations of human nature within it is more readily able to engage with postmodern sensibilities, particularly the interest in *eros*, than earlier, more liberal-inclined, twentieth-century approaches. Contrary to the openness to Kant in some neo-Thomist accounts of natural law, McAleer believes that if St. Thomas were alive today, he would join in with the postmodern attacks on Kantian rationality.[69]

McAleer is also critical of the political dimensions of the Maritain project. He suggests that "rather than arguing that natural law is a controlling framework for the Catholic adoption of the Rights of Man and

---

[63] McAleer, *Ecstatic Morality and Sexual Politics*, 14.

[64] For a sympathetic but critical review of this work, see J. Heffernan Schindler, "The Metaphysics of Love," *The Review of Politics* 69 (Winter 2007): 301–04.

[65] McAleer, *Ecstatic Morality and Sexual Politics*, 81.

[66] Ibid., 93.

[67] Ibid., 63.

[68] Ibid., 15.

[69] Ibid., 21.

democracy, as Maritain promoted it, it would be better to understand natural law as a framework of privilege."[70] This is because the "logic of rights has for its *raison d'être* an equalitarianism that is at root a horror of privilege and its protection of diversity."[71] Catholic teaching on sex and marriage also relies upon ideas of privilege and hierarchy.[72]

Moreover, Maritain's project has been turned against the Church by contemporary liberals who argue that the attempted baptism of American-style liberalism inherent within it was but the first stage in what should be a more total democratic revolution encompassing the areas of sexuality and ecclesiology. McAleer believes that the Church cannot do this because her thinking on these two topics (sexuality and ecclesiology) is deeply Christological. In this context, McAleer's work is on the same trajectory as that of Robert P. Kraynak, who has also argued that Catholic scholars play a dangerous game when they baptize democracy as if it were an absolute good in one context and then attempt to defend hierarchical privileges in others.[73] However, whereas Kraynak has generally looked to the Augustinian tradition to provide antidotes for the political influence of Maritain, McAleer is recommending the thought of Aurel Kolnai (1900–1973), whose anti-utopian disposition and concerns about totalitarian tendencies within the liberal tradition resonate well with the Augustinian reserve toward the notion of a perfect social order.[74] McAleer concludes that the values inherent in papal encyclicals such as *Veritatis Splendor* and *Evangelium Vitae* are "better defended through Aurel Kolnai's thought, for social and political privilege are more congruent with the Christological body than are the isolationism and decisionism of rights."[75] When placed within the framework of nuptial mysticism, morality becomes a matter of desiring to be more like Christ.

---

[70] Ibid., 161.

[71] Ibid.

[72] Ibid., 176.

[73] Robert P. Kraynak, *Christian Faith and Modern Democracy: God and Politics in a Fallen World* (Notre Dame, IN: University of Notre Dame Press, 2001).

[74] Kolnai came to academic prominence in the 1930s as a contributor of anti-Nazi articles to Dietrich von Hildebrand's *Der Österreichische Ständestaat* and as the author of *The War against the West* (1938). After fleeing Austria, he spent the 1940s and half of the 1950s at the University of Laval, where he found the regnant neo-Thomism insufferable. For a survey of Kolnai's thought, see Daniel Mahoney, "Recovery of the Common World: An Introduction to the Moral and Political Reflections of Aurel Kolnai," in *Privilege and Liberty and Other Essays in Political Philosophy* (Lanham, MD: Lexington Books, 1999).

[75] McAleer, *Ecstatic Morality and Sexual Politics*, 171.

The conclusion to be drawn from the above brief survey of recent scholarship on natural law doctrine is that Catholic scholars need to go beyond a theologically neutered conception of natural law as a *lingua franca* with which to engage proponents of hostile traditions. However, nothing in the above should be construed as a call to abandon the Church's mission to those whom MacIntyre calls "plain persons" who tacitly adopt the attitudes of the elite as they filter through and undergird the practices of the institutions in which they live and work. Rather, what is being argued is that the Church's scholars should not waste their energies performing all manner of linguistic gymnastics, transposing her teachings into the idioms of hostile traditions, in order to entice neo-pagan elites to buy their intellectual package.

The movement from a neo-Thomist account of natural law to one that explicitly acknowledges its Trinitarian context is unlikely to make the notion of natural law any less acceptable to such elites. If they oppose a more liberal-sounding version of it, then one might as well drop this project and concentrate on making the teaching more comprehensible and attractive to the Catholic faithful and plain persons of goodwill, especially Protestants.[76] Further work also needs to be done in recovering lost ground with those who are nominally Catholic and have never been presented with a comprehensive account of morality as filial participation in the life and love of the Trinity.

The work of providing a richer account of the natural law doctrine from within the nuptial mysticism framework may also have the effect of reconciling tensions between the younger generation of Catholic scholars working within the Thomist and Balthasarian traditions. In particular, it has been suggested above that the work of Pinckaers might stand as a bridge uniting the efforts of younger Thomists and Balthasarians because of its accent on the theo-dramatic nature of moral life, and also because of Pinckaers's sympathy to the work of de Lubac, which one finds in his licentiate dissertation and several subsequent essays.[77]

---

[76] The works of Ulrich Kühn and Per-Erik Persson are evidence of an interest in natural law (rooted in Trinitarian anthropology) from within the Lutheran tradition, and the work of David Novak on Old Testament ethics exhibits a significant interest in natural law from within the Jewish tradition, which, though obviously not linked to a Trinitarian anthropology, at least shares some of the elements of a Christian cosmology. There is much potential for successful diplomatic work with members of the Protestant communities who have been encouraged by the Christocentric accent of the moral theology of the current and previous pontificates.

[77] Servais-Théodore Pinckaers, *Le "surnaturel" du P. de Lubac* (La Sarte: STL Thesis, 1952).

The future direction of natural law scholarship would thus seem to be framed by this question: In what way(s) do the differences between Baroque Thomist and Lubacian-Balthasarian accounts of the Trinitarian relationships and the grace–nature relationship impact upon the development of an account of natural law rooted within the theological anthropology of *Gaudium et Spes* §22?[78] Can one indeed have an account of natural law linked to the theological anthropology of *Gaudium et Spes* §22 without adopting at least some of the elements of de Lubac's criticisms of Baroque Thomism?

The strategic and political question also remains of how to engage intellectually with proponents of the liberal tradition. The argument presented in this paper is that whatever the answer to that question, the attempted transposition of natural law into liberal idioms favored by Maritain and others in his tradition should be re-assessed against the empirical sociological data and legal and political history of the past four decades. Perhaps a better way to engage with liberals is to move the discussion away from nature, reason, and natural law and toward the idioms of freedom, self-development, and self-realization, to offer an immanent critique, as it were, of particular liberal policy proposals. One example of a Catholic political philosopher who has approached the liberal tradition in this manner is the Jagiellonian professor Ryszard Legutko, whose essays such as "Do Liberals Love Liberty?" and "The Temptation of Total Laissez-Faire" provide concrete examples of this strategy.[79]

---

[78] The term "Baroque Thomist" refers to contemporary Thomists who continue to accept as authoritative the accounts of the grace–nature relationship as presented by Cajetan and Thomists of the sixteenth-century Salamanca School.

[79] See: Ryszard Legutko, *Dylematy Kapitalizmu*, Biblioteka Libertas 2 (Paris: Editions Spotkania, 1986); Legutko, "Do Liberals Love Liberty?" *Salisbury Review* 7, no. 1 (September 1988); Legutko, *Society as a Department Store* (Lanham, MD: Lexington Books, 2002); Legutko, *On Tolerance: A Study of Strong Government, Law of Nature, Love and Conscience* (Krakow: Centre for Political Thought, 1997); Legutko, *The Demon in Democracy: Totalitarian Temptations in Free Societies* (New York: Encounter Books, 2016).

CHAPTER 9

The Humanism of the Incarnation: Catholic, Barthian, and Dutch Reformed[1]

THE FOLLOWING ESSAY takes the form of a reflection on the idea of the "humanism of the Incarnation" in which the "participant" voices will principally be those of Martin D'Arcy, Charles Journet, Karol Wojtyła, Joseph Ratzinger, and Marc Ouellet representing the Catholic academy, Karl Barth representing himself, and Abraham Kuyper representing the Dutch Reformed tradition.

Martin D'Arcy (1888–1978) was a twentieth-century English Jesuit renowned for converting a rather large number of Oxford undergraduates, including Evelyn Waugh. He is said to have been the inspiration for the character of Fr. Rothschild in Waugh's novel *Vile Bodies*. Several chapters of his book *The Sense of History: Secular and Sacred* offer a mid-twentieth-century engagement with Karl Barth's ideas on what is now called "the theology of culture." D'Arcy in turn was influenced by an essay of Christopher Butler, who was Abbot of Downside Abbey. Butler's article "The Value of History" was published in the *Downside Review* in 1950, and he himself was following leads in the work of the Belgian Jesuit Léopold Malevez (1900–1973), whose work is known for its identification of a division between incarnational and eschatological approaches to history. For those who favor the eschatological approach, the emphasis is on the discontinu-

---

[1]   This essay was first presented as part of the Robert Louis Wilken Ecumenical Symposium at Baylor University, Waco, TX, February 1, 2013, and first published in *Nova et Vetera* (English) 13, no. 1 (2015): 125–54.

ity between profane history and the final reign of God after the renewal of the cosmos, while for those who favor the incarnational approach, the general idea is that all good human actions prepare for the coming age beyond the consummation of the world.[2] The eschatological approach is usually identified with an emphasis on the theology of the Cross, while the incarnational approach is identified, obviously, with the theology of the Incarnation. Malevez had been influenced by a fellow Belgian theologian, Gustave Thils (1909–2000), who was a *peritus* at the Second Vatican Council and a member of the Secretariat for Christian Unity. Thils is generally remembered for his doctrinal history of the ecumenical movement published in 1955 and for his criticism of the theology of Jean Daniélou for being too far down the eschatological end of the spectrum.[3]

The other Catholic voices to be mentioned are Charles Journet (1891–1975), a Swiss cardinal associated with the journal *Nova et Vetera*, Jean Borella, a contemporary French theologian, Joseph Ratzinger, who needs no introduction, and Marc Ouellet, the Canadian who was given the shortest odds of any cardinal entering the 2013 conclave by Paddy Powers's Irish betting agency.

Abraham Kuyper (1837–1920), representing the Dutch Reformed tradition, was Prime Minister of the Netherlands from 1901 to 1905 and the founder of a newspaper, a university, a political party, and a religious denomination. His most famous academic works are his *Lectures on Calvinism*, first delivered at Princeton Seminary in 1898. The Princeton seminary now hosts the Abraham Kuyper Center for Public Theology and sponsors the annual Kuyper Prize Lecture, as well as publishing *The Kuyper Centre Review*. My judgment of Kuyper is that he was a kind of Calvinist Alasdair MacIntyre—that is to say, he was someone keenly interested in the relationship between theological ideas and culture and he was decidedly anti-liberal. Just as MacIntyre encourages the formation of small institutions governed by persons who all share the same theological framework, Kuyper is remembered as a champion of "pillarization," the sociological term given to the denominational segregation of pre-World War II Dutch society.

A fellow Calvinist, though in a tradition all his own, Karl Barth

---

2   This is Abbott Christopher Butler's summary of the distinction in "The Value of History," *Downside Review* 68, no. 213 (Summer 1950): 290–305, at 290–91. For the original analysis by Malevez, see Léopold Malevez, "Deux théologies catholiques de l'histoire," *Bijdragen* 10 (1949): 225–40.

3   Gustave Thils, *Histoire Doctrinale du Mouvement Oecuménique* (Louvain: Em. Warny, 1955).

(1886–1968) was, to quote Pope Pius XII, "the most important theologian since Thomas Aquinas." Barth was invited to be an observer at the Second Vatican Council and later published a work of reflections on the documents of the Council entitled *Ad Limina Apostolorum*: *A Reappraisal of Vatican II*. In 1966, when he met Pope Paul VI, he asked the pontiff what one might colloquially call the billion-dollar question: what does *aggiornamento* mean, accommodation to what?[4]

Aggiornamento was the 1960s buzzword for theological renewal, also translated as "updating," which mutated into "accommodating." It was closely related to the post-conciliar pastoral strategy known as "correlationism," the idea that the faith needed to be correlated to the culture of the times. As the French Dominican Marie-Dominique Chenu (1895–1990) described the idea, one needed to look to the contemporary culture for *pierres d'attente*, or toothing stones, to which the faith could attach itself. This pastoral strategy was strongly associated with the post-conciliar theology of the Flemish Dominican Edward Schillebeeckx (1914–2009), and it had a major impact on the direction of Catholic ecclesial life throughout the pontificate of Paul VI (1963–1978). For many clergy educated in Catholic seminaries in the 1960s, the correlationist project remains synonymous with the "spirit of the Council."

When applied in the 1960s, 70s, and 80s, "correlationism" came to mean accommodating the faith to the culture of modernity. Today, proponents of this project (found mostly in the Netherlands and Belgium) argue that instead of correlating the faith to the culture of modernity, ecclesial leaders need to "recontextualize" the faith to the culture of postmodernity. This is because the culture of modernity and its "modern man" are now regarded as the undesirable refuse of the eighteenth century. The "modern man" has been variously described as a "one-dimensional man" (by the Frankfurt School's Herbert Marcuse), an *animal producens et consumens* (by the Czech Jesuit Joseph Zverina), a "mass man" who has "no desire for independence or originality" (by Germany's Romano Guardini), a "deprived and isolated emotivist" (the assessment of Alasdair MacIntyre), a "micro-cosmic tragedy" (the term used by the Slovakian, Charter-77 anti-Communist activist Rudolf Battek), a person with a weak or fractured sense of self-identity who "doesn't know which team he is playing on" (the assessment of the Czech writer and politician Václav Havel), a Hobbesian egoist (the label of the English philosopher John Gray), and a new type of barbarian (the conclusion of the Czech philosopher Erazim Kohak), to

---

[4]   Karl Barth, *Ad Limina Apostolorum* (Edinburgh: St. Andrews Press, 1969), 20.

mention just a few of the descriptions.[5] When one adds the Nietzschean definitions as someone with a "small soul" and "herd-like morality" and communitarian criticisms of the "rootless cosmopolitan"—a being without any historical memory and without loyalties to any traditions—one rapidly reaches the conclusion that the depiction of anyone as a "modern" and the endorsement of the culture of modernity as the natural habitat of these neobarbaric, microcosmic tragedies carry strong negative connotations. This is so not only for Catholic scholars but also for Heideggerians like Václav Havel and members of the Frankfurt school like Herbert Marcuse. To use the language of marketing managers, modernity is toxic.

Whether one is correlating or recontextualizing, either way, it is something else that is positioning the faith—in effect, something else that is positioning Christ.[6] One might say that, if onto-theology is bad (allowing philosophy to position revelation), then *zeitgeist* theology is even worse. There is a huge difference between using contemporary cultural trends as a standard for the analysis of revelation and using revelation as a lens through which to read and judge contemporary cultural trends. Arguably, it is these alternative ways of engaging with the spirit of the times that determine whether one is a liberal or non-liberal theologian, and all of the authors addressed in this paper share the quality of being non-liberal theologians. They are also all strongly Christocentric, and the question to be posed is "what is their vision of a Christian humanism—or to use Ratzinger's expression, the 'humanism of the Incarnation?'"

My macrolevel observation is that there seems to be broad agreement on two fundamental principles: first, that any humanism of the Incarnation presupposes a theology of creation and a theology of the Cross and is set within these two poles; and second, that, in relation to the Incarnation itself, Christology becomes the all-important point of reference. These

---

[5]   Herbert Marcuse, *One Dimensional Man* (Boston: Beacon Press, 1964); Jozef Zverina, as quoted by Rudolf Battek, "Spiritual Values, Independent Initiatives and Politics," in *The Power of the Powerless*, ed. John Keane (London: Hutchinson, 1985), 97–99; Romano Guardini, *The End of the Modern World* (London: Sheed & Ward, 1957); Alasdair MacIntyre, *After Virtue: A Study in Moral Theory* (London: Duckworth, 1981); Václav Havel, "Politics and Conscience," *Salisbury Review* 2 (January 1985); John Gray, *Liberalism* (London: Open University Press, 1986); Erazim Kohak, *The Embers and the Stars: A Philosophical Inquiry into the Moral Sense of Nature* (Chicago: University of Chicago, 1984).

[6]   Robert Barron, *The Priority of Christ: Toward a Post-Liberal Catholicism* (Grand Rapids, MI: Brazos Press, 2007), 341: "I have argued in *The Priority of Christ* that Jesus and the doctrines and narratives surrounding him must have epistemic primacy, that is, to say, they cannot be interpreted or positioned by anything outside of themselves."

two principles appear to apply across the various faith traditions. This means in turn that to do justice to this topic, one needs to be across the Christology of the authors surveyed, and this in turn means being across their Trinitarian theology and then applying both to their understanding of the relationship between Christ and humanity and human culture. The topic is therefore sufficiently deep to justify a doctoral level analysis, and thus, what follows in this paper is merely a typical first chapter of a doctoral literature review. It is nonetheless important because, if there is to be an ecumenical united front against the forces of atheism and its culture of death, then it helps to understand not only what we are all against but, positively, what we all want to foster.

In an article on the interventions of Cardinal Josef Frings in the debates of the Second Vatican Council, Joseph Ratzinger observed that Frings was keen to emphasize one general principle: "For the Christian life in the world three revealed truths are always to be kept before us: creation, which teaches us to love the things of the world as God's work; the Incarnation, which spurs us on to dedicate to God all the things of the world; the cross and resurrection, which leads us in the imitation of Christ to sacrifice and continence with regard to the things of the world."[7] An almost identical point was made in a summary of the position of Dietrich Bonhoeffer by Jens Zimmermann: "[I]n Jesus Christ we believe in the God who became human, was crucified, and is risen. In the becoming human we recognize God's love towards God's creation, in the crucifixion God's judgment of all flesh, and in the resurrection God's purpose for a new world. Nothing could be more perverse than to tear these three apart because the whole is contained in each of them."[8]

Consistent with Frings, Ratzinger, Bonhoeffer, and Zimmermann, Abbot Christopher Butler made the point that Christian eschatology and Christian incarnationalism are not mutually exclusive and that the division identified by Léopold Malevez between the two in their approaches to history should not be a real division, but rather two poles held in tension:

> Eschatology without Incarnation is not Christian at all, but Jewish. Incarnation without eschatology is—I know not what; Bud-

---

[7] Joseph Ratzinger, "Frings's Speeches During the Second Vatican Council: Apropos of A. Muggeridge's *The Desolate City*," *Communio: International Catholic Review* 15, no. 1 (1988):131–47.

[8] Jens Zimmermann, *Incarnational Humanism: A Philosophy of Culture for the Church in the World* (Westmont, IL: InterVarsity Press, 2012), 273.

dhism, perhaps, or Platonism. Born within the Jewish tradition and of Jewish spiritual stock, Christianity has been eschatological from the beginning. . . . But its novelty was not that it simply lodged the idea of incarnation within an eschatological frame-work, but that it proclaimed a real, "mystical," "sacramental" anticipation of the Last Things as the unique gift that God was bestowing on man in the Gospel—and of this real anticipation the Incarnation is the epitome and the fountainhead. . . . Incarnation, for us, is eschatological, and eschatology is incarnated.[9]

The confessional difficulty here, of course, is found in the phrase "sacramental anticipation of the Last Things." Not all Christian faith traditions will agree that the humanism of the Incarnation is something rooted in a sacramental ontology. This seems to be the neuralgic point of dispute between the Catholic and Protestant visions, and the subject of some acute comments by Charles Journet. In his work *The Primacy of Peter*, Journet distinguished between two different concepts of Christianity, one typical of Protestant theology and one typical of Catholic theology. The first he described as the "mnemic concept," the second as "the ontological concept." The difference between the two is presented as a difference over the way in which the presence of Christ constitutes Christianity:

On the one hand there is the spirituality of the Incarnation, or in a broader sense the spirituality of the transfiguration of matter by the spirit. This is the Catholic form of spirituality with its doctrine of the Incarnation, the instrumental causality of the sacraments, of the New Law, the visibility of the Church, the resurrection of the flesh, the immediate creation of visible things by God himself, etc. On the other hand, we have a sort of spirituality of disincarnation, or in a broader sense a spirituality of the separation of matter and spirit.

On a more metaphysical plane we may see the opposition as one between a dogmatic view of the analogy of being, in accordance with which the divine privileges, especially divine sanctity, can be communicated analogically to creatures—as existence once was—without affecting adversely the divine transcendence, but rather manifesting it. On the other hand we have a dogmatic view of the uniqueness of being, which can only safeguard the di-

---

9   Butler, "The Value of History," 294.

vine transcendence by denying any possibility for the divine privileges to be communicated, especially divine sanctity: either a) to
the humanity of Christ because of the fear of Monophysitism, or
b) to creatures because of the fear of idolatry.[10]

According to Journet, in the Protestant account, Christ is only present in
time by way of signs, tokens, and promises. From a Catholic point of view,
this would be a kind of nostalgic return to the Old Testament because
the Catholic account sees Christ as really and truly present in time under
the guise of signs, tokens, and promises. Journet suggests that Protestantism makes the error of considering the two natures of Christ side by side
such that the human nature of Christ becomes "simply an occasion of our
salvation, a mere phenomenal shell, in which the invisible God made his
appearance."[11]

While Journet does not distinguish between different Protestant traditions but lumps them all together and comes rather close to describing
Protestant Christology as Nestorian, in another work, *The Sense of the Supernatural*, Jean Borella specifically indicted the Lutheran tradition in the
charge of monothelitism (that human nature becomes a pure instrument
of divine nature without autonomy):

> Basically, and whatever may have been his [Luther's] good inten-
> tions, [his] thesis rests on the radical incompatibility of nature
> and grace, or rather on the irreducible opposition and the mutu-
> al exclusion of the natural and supernatural orders, which grace
> comes to reconcile specifically, since this grace always flows from
> the unique hypostasis of Christ in which divinity has been unit-
> ed to humanity. Here, to the contrary [that is, in the Lutheran
> tradition], supernature can only work by destroying nature. . . .
> Into the heart of every Christian it introduces an insurmount-
> able separation between what stems from the creature and what
> stems from the redemptive act. . . . What disappears in this way is
> the "immanence of grace" of Christ the Redeemer in his creation;
> that is, the sacramental and ritual order, the ecclesial order, the
> Mystical Body, all of this sacralizing of the earthly and the human
> cosmos which is the Incarnation prolonged, spread abroad and

---

[10] Charles Journet, *The Primacy of Peter* (Westminster, MD: Newman Press, 1954), 36–
37.

[11] Ibid., 33.

communicated, as the image of the first fruits of the "new heaven and the new earth."[12]

Although Borella was directing his comments to the Lutheran tradition, they would seem to apply equally to the theological vision of Barth. For Barth, it is Christ, not the Church, who mediates the presence of God to the world. As Rodney Howsare expresses the point, "missing [from Barth] is the more Eastern understanding that God unites himself, in the incarnation, to all human nature, thereby transforming the capacities of that nature. This comes out most clearly in Barth's understanding of the Church, the liturgy and the sacraments."[13] Howsare also explains that, "by reducing everything to God's activity in Christ on behalf of the world, Barth does not give the same attention and emphasis to the role of the Church's indispensable role in carrying this love into the world"—as Catholic theologians typically do—"[and so] missing from Barth's picture is a notion of the Church as itself a sacrament."[14] Barth is generally believed to have held a neo-Zwinglian position on the sacraments, or at least that is the strong impression he gives in his *Church Dogmatics* IV/4. For Barth, both baptism and the Lord's Supper are human actions, not sacraments. Louis-Marie Chauvet argues that Barth's Christology already bears within itself its nonsacramental theology. Chauvet remarks that there are few theologies that speak so much of events and history and, yet, there are few theologies where so little takes place on the properly historical plane.[15]

It was perhaps for these reasons that Hans Urs von Balthasar accused Barth of reducing the order of creation to the order of grace.[16] In Balthasar's words: "If revelation is centered in Jesus Christ, there must be by definition a periphery to this center. Thus, as we say, the order of the Incarnation presupposes the order of creation, which is not identical with it. And, because the order of creation is oriented to the order of the Incarnation, it is structured in view of the Incarnation: it contains images, as it were, dispositions,

---

[12] Jean Borella, *The Sense of the Supernatural* (Edinburgh: T & T Clark, 1998), 154.

[13] Rodney A. Howsare, *Hans Urs von Balthasar: The Ecumenical Implications of His Theological Style* (Edinburgh: T & T Clark, 2005), 97.

[14] Ibid., 92.

[15] Louis-Marie Chauvet, *Symbol and Sacrament: A Sacramental Reinterpretation of Christian Existence* (Collegeville, MN: Liturgical Press, 1995), 540.

[16] Hans Urs von Balthasar, *The Theology of Karl Barth* (San Francisco: Ignatius Press, 1992), 136.

which in a true sense are the presuppositions for the Incarnation."[17] In other words, the idea is that the grace available through Jesus Christ does not stand in contradiction to, but in line with, the grace found in nature by virtue of God's act of creation.

Michael Schmaus, a professor of the Theology Faculty in Munich during Ratzinger's student years, expressed the general Catholic idea like this:

> Man exists, not in himself, but for God. By directing himself in free decision and responsibility to God, he acts according to his ontic constitution, he acts in the way appropriate to his essence and thus comes to fulfil and perfect his being. Only when God draws him into his own triune life does man find his own deepest being; his ontic determination is a copy of God's tri-personal life. Thus man comes to discover himself in the divine Thou when God imparts himself to him supernaturally. This communication of God's happens in and through Christ. The relationship to Christ is therefore contained in the relationship of the creature to God. . . . The whole of the rest of creation is meant to exist for the sake of the Incarnation of Christ. Thus the whole of creation comes to its essential fulfilment only through him.[18]

Ratzinger's own most extensive and unbuttoned treatment of this topic can be found in an article published in 1969 in Herbert Vorgrimler's *Commentaries on the Documents of the Second Vatican Council*. The article analyzed the treatment of human dignity in *Gaudium et Spes*, the Pastoral Constitution on the Church in the Modern World. Ratzinger's assessment of this document was largely negative, agreeing with Walter Kasper that the first section of the document was never properly integrated with the second. The first section offers an account of the human person as made in God's image, but it is only when one gets to §22 that the picture is complicated by the introduction of the Trinity. Ratzinger argued that the first section fostered the fiction that it is possible to construct a rational philosophical picture of man intelligible to all and on which all men of goodwill can agree, the actual Christian doctrines being added to this as a sort of crowning conclusion. This approach prompted the question of "why exactly the reasonable and perfectly free human being described in

---

[17] Ibid., 163.
[18] Michael Schmaus, *Katholische Dogmatik II* (Munich: Max Hueber, 1949), 70–72.

the first articles was suddenly burdened with the story of Christ."[19]

Notwithstanding this criticism and Ratzinger's description of the language used in the paragraph about human freedom as downright Pelagian, he nonetheless strongly praised §22, which was to become the most often quoted paragraphs of all the documents of the Second Vatican Council by John Paul II. He said that, in §22, the idea of Christ's assumption of human nature is touched upon in its full ontological depth: "The human nature of all men is one; Christ's taking to himself the one human nature of man is an event which affects every human being; consequently human nature in every human being is henceforward Christologically characterized." Ratzinger went on to say that this outlook is important because it opens a bridge between the theology of the Incarnation and that of the Cross: "A theology of the incarnation situated too much on the level of essence, may be tempted to be satisfied with the ontological phenomenon: God's being and man's have been conjoined. . . . But since it is made clear that man's being is not that of a pure essence, and that he only attains his reality by his activity, it is at once evident that we cannot rest content with a purely essentialist outlook. Man's being must therefore be examined precisely in its activities."[20]

Here Ratzinger is opening up what in other places he has referred to as the mediation of history in the realm of ontology. He and Karol Wojtyła converge in their interest in the uniqueness of human persons caused by their particular location within history. For this reason, they share a mutual interest in what is called relationality, or that dimension of the human person that is determined by his or her relations with other persons, including the Persons of the Holy Trinity. In another essay on the "Notion of the Human Person" published during the pontificate of John Paul II, Ratzinger was critical of the Boethian definition of the person as the individual substance of a rational nature because it neglected the whole dimension of relationality that makes human persons not merely members of the human race but unique individual members of the human race.[21] Both Wojtyła and Ratzinger were driven to develop this dimension of Catholic anthropology as a response to issues thrown up by existentialist philosophy. A theology that has nothing to say about indi-

---

[19] Ibid., 120.

[20] Joseph Ratzinger, "The Dignity of the Human Person," in *Commentary on the Documents of the Second Vatican Council*, vol. 5, ed. Herbert Vorgrimler (London: Burns and Oates, 1969), 160.

[21] Joseph Ratzinger, "Concerning the Notion of Person in Theology," *Communio* 17, no. 3 (1990): 439–54.

viduality is impotent against the power of nineteenth-century German romanticism and its twentieth-century developments.

Ratzinger believes that the uniqueness of Christian culture is rooted in the Incarnation and that all of its specific characteristics disintegrate when this belief is eclipsed.[22] The Incarnation means that the invisible God enters into the visible world so that those who are bound to matter can know him. The International Theological Commission, under Ratzinger's leadership, expressed the position in the following paragraph:

> In the last times inaugurated at Pentecost, the risen Christ, Alpha and Omega, enters into the history of peoples: from that moment, the sense of history and thus of culture is unsealed and the Holy Spirit reveals it by actualizing and communicating it to all. The Church is the sacrament of this revelation and its communication. It re-centers every culture into which Christ is received, placing it in the axis of the world which is coming, and restores the union broken by the Prince of this world. Culture is thus eschatologically situated; it tends towards its completion in Christ, but it cannot be saved except by associating itself with the repudiation of evil.[23]

In this paragraph, one finds all the key elements of a Catholic incarnational humanism and its associate culture: the Incarnation restores the union broken by Satan at the time of the Fall; it re-centers culture eschatologically (that is, with a view to the return of Christ in glory and consummation of the world); but this does not happen automatically. There needs to be a repudiation of evil, and thus, the potentiality of the Incarnation stands always under the shadow of the Cross. The Holy Spirit and the Church are responsible for the communication of the possibilities thrown open by the Incarnation to the world.

For the development of a more detailed Catholic Christocentric Trinitarian anthropology, one can have recourse to John Paul II's encyclicals *Redemptor Hominis* (1979), *Dives in Misericordia* (1980), and *Dominum et Vivificantem* (1986). In this "Trinitarian triptych," each of these encyclicals addressed the issue of the human person's relationship with one of the Persons of the Holy Trinity. Included in this Trinitarian anthropology is the notion that the Incarnation opened up the possibility

---

[22] Joseph Ratzinger, *Co-Workers of the Truth* (San Francisco: Ignatius Press, 1992), 18–19.

[23] International Theological Commission, "Faith and Inculturation," *Origins* 18 (1989): 800–07.

of participation in the very life of God, which John Paul II addressed in *Dives in Misericordia* §7.

The same idea is often expressed by the idea of the nuptial mystery. An extensive presentation of the links between Eucharistic theology and the nuptial mystery can be found in Pope Benedict's Apostolic Exhortation *Sacramentum Caritatis* at §27:

> The Eucharist, as the sacrament of charity, has a particular relationship with the love of man and woman united in marriage. . . . "the entire Christian life bears the mark of the spousal love of Christ and the Church. Already Baptism, the entry into the People of God, is a nuptial mystery; it is so to speak the nuptial bath which precedes the wedding feast, the Eucharist." . . . By the power of the sacrament, the marriage bond is intrinsically linked to the eucharistic unity of Christ the Bridegroom and his Bride, the Church (cf. *Eph* 5:31–32). The mutual consent that husband and wife exchange in Christ, which establishes them as a community of life and love, also has a eucharistic dimension. Indeed, in the theology of Saint Paul, conjugal love is a sacramental sign of Christ's love for his Church, a love culminating in the Cross, the expression of his "marriage" with humanity and at the same time the origin and heart of the Eucharist.

These themes have been amplified in the theology of Cardinal Marc Ouellet who understands the sacrament of marriage, including the exchange of love between husband and wife, as the couple's participation in the exchange of "gifts" between the divine Persons:

> God's covenant with Israel and humanity is the story of a wedding. The symbol par excellence of the biblical revelation is conjugal love. A couple stands at the beginning of salvation history and another at its conclusion: Adam and Eve set the history of humanity in motion, while the Lamb and his Bride, who descends from God in heaven, concludes the adventure of historical time. In the span of time between the initial couple and the eschatological couple, the Holy Spirit implores and summons; he prays for the final fulfillment together with the Bride whom he has called.[24]

---

[24] Marc Ouellet, *Divine Likeness: Towards a Trinitarian Anthropology of the Family* (Grand Rapids, MI: Eerdmans, 2006), 80.

> Salvation history is [thus] a spousal drama of Trinitarian revelation. . . . The Father sends his Son as the Bridegroom, accompanied by the Holy Spirit, who prepares the bride for the encounter with the Bridegroom and the fulfilment of the eschatological wedding.[25]

> Prepared by the Holy Spirit since the beginning of creation, the messianic wedding is celebrated on the altar of the Cross. It is precisely there that the nuptial chamber receives the *sacrum commercium et conubium*.[26]

Ouellet concludes that the Paschal event contains at once a Trinitarian and a spousal meaning: "A Trinitarian meaning, since the resurrection seals in the economy the unity of love which was sealed by the Holy Spirit's procession in the immanent Trinity: a spousal meaning, because this anointing confirmation seals the fecund gift of the risen one as the eschatological Bridegroom who generates his bride."[27]

These notions of a spousal relation between Christ and the Church and of divine filiation via sacramental participation in the life and love of the Trinity are elements found in most Catholic accounts of the humanism of the Incarnation, but they are usually missing from Protestant accounts, and in particular from Barth's. In his book *Karl Barth's Theology of Culture*, Robert J. Palma speaks of Barth's "parabolic relationship between the worldly and the heavenly, the human and the divine, the transitory and the eternal."[28] Thus, we might say, in shorthand terms, there is a tendency for Catholic theologians to describe the union between the human person and the Persons of the Holy Trinity using the idioms of nuptial mysticism, while there is a tendency for Protestants to shy away from this and adopt a more modest notion of a parabolic relationship. For Barth, the eschatological Word to which Christianity looks forward relativizes all historical possibilities and achievements. Though his later theology expressed the point more gently, Barth never retracted his early claim that only a thoroughly eschatological Christianity bears any relationship to Christ.[29]

The difference in the area of sacramental theology also means that

---

[25] Ibid., 80–81.

[26] Ibid., 85.

[27] Ibid., 87.

[28] Robert J. Palma, *Karl Barth's Theology of Culture* (Eugene, OR: Pickwick, 1983), 2.

[29] Gary Dorrien, "The 'Postmodern' Barth? The Word of God as True Myth," *The Christian Century* 114, no. 11 (1997): 338–42.

Protestants and Catholics tend to have a different attitude toward matter itself, including the human body. The Catholic cult of the saints and practice of collecting and venerating the relics of the saints is the most obvious example of this difference. Theologically, the issue is one of understanding precisely how it is that Christ unites himself to humanity. That Christ was not some kind of ontological exception, but that his Incarnation affected all post-lapsarian human nature in some way, comes across strongly in John Paul II's encyclical *Dominum et Vivificantem*, in which, at §50, he wrote:

> The Incarnation of God the Son signifies the taking up into the unity with God not only of human nature, but in this human nature, in a sense, of everything that is "flesh": the whole of humanity, the entire visible and material world. The Incarnation then, also has a cosmic significance, a cosmic dimension. The "first-born of all creation," becoming incarnate in the individual humanity of Christ, unites himself in some way with the entire reality of man, which is "flesh"—and in this reality with all "flesh," with the whole of creation.

This Catholic take on the Incarnation would seem to affect not only issues like how we treat the dead bodies of the saints but attitudes toward art and culture more generally. In a reflection on the earliest disputes within the Church about art and beauty, Ratzinger observed that "iconoclasm rests on a one-sided apophatic theology, which recognizes only the Wholly Other-ness of the God beyond all images and words, a theology that in the final analysis regards revelation as the inadequate human reflection of what is eternally imperceptible."[30] He concluded that "what seems like the highest humility toward God turns into pride, allowing God no word and permitting him no real entry into history. . . . Matter is absolutized and thought of as completely impervious to God, as mere matter, and thus deprived of its dignity."[31]

This notion of the receptivity of matter to some form of divinization reaches its most dramatic expression in §11 of Benedict's *Sacramentum Caritatis*: "The substantial conversion of bread and wine into [Christ's] body and blood introduces within creation the principle of a radical change, a sort of 'nuclear fission,' which penetrates to the heart of all being, a change meant to set off a process which transforms reality, a process

---

[30] Joseph Ratzinger, *The Spirit of the Liturgy* (San Francisco: Ignatius Press, 2000), 124.
[31] Ibid.

leading ultimately to the transfiguration of the entire world, to the point where God will be all in all (cf. *1 Cor* 15:28)." The theology of Teilhard de Chardin, in particular the idea that as we move through history, matter itself becomes more and more conformed to Christ until we reach the "Noosphere," as he called it, has never received magisterial endorsement, but the fact that a significant Catholic theologian could speculate in this way is evidence of the depth of Catholic interest in the topic of what it means exactly for the world to be transfigured to a point where God will be all in all.

In addition to the different stances toward sacramental theology and the theological meaning of the first chapter of St. Paul's *Letter to the Corinthians*, Ratzinger's humanism of the Incarnation also differs from Barth's in that he believes that Mariology has something to contribute to this topic:

> Mariology is an essential component of a hermeneutics of salvation history. Recognition of this fact brings out the true dimensions of Christology over against a falsely understood *solus Christus* [Christ alone]. Christology must speak of a Christ who is both "head *and* body," that is, who comprises the redeemed creation in its relative subsistence [*Selbständigkeit*]. But this move simultaneously enlarges our perspective beyond the history of salvation, because it counters a false understanding of God's sole agency, highlighting the reality of the creature that God calls and enables to respond to him freely. Mariology demonstrates that the doctrine of grace does not revoke creation, but is the definitive Yes to creation. In this way, Mariology guarantees the ontological independence [*Eigenständigkeit*] of creation, undergirds faith in creation, and crowns the doctrine of creation, rightly understood.[32]

The nexus between Christology and versions of Christian humanism is acknowledged in almost all the authorities who write about this topic in the work of Karl Barth, and it is the central theme of Paul Louis Metzger's work *The Word of Christ and the World of Culture: Sacred and Secular through the Theology of Karl Barth*. However, there appears to be no consensus among the Barthian scholars about how to read Barth's Christology, and there has been a debate within the school about whether Barth

---

[32] Joseph Ratzinger, *Mary: The Church at the Source* (San Francisco: Ignatius Press, 2005), 31.

was primarily an Alexandrian or an Antiochene. According to George Hunsinger of the Princeton Theological Seminary, who wrote the chapter on Barth's Christology for the *Cambridge Companion to Barth*, Barth does have a Chalcedonian Christology but he arrives at it by moving back and forth dialectically between the Alexandrian and Antiochene approaches.[33] However, according to Charles T. Waldrop, in Barth, "Christ's human nature is so integrally taken up and assumed into God's being that its purely human existence is denied. In the final analysis, the degree of independence which the human nature has is extremely slight. It serves and attests God because God determines it to be that which serves and attests him."[34] Whatever is made of the differences between Hunsinger and Waldrop, Metzger strongly argues that, for Barth, the human constitution has no inherent capacity for the divine capacity.[35] Nor, if we are good Barthians, should we expect to find vestiges of the Trinity within creation.[36] Instead, Barth invented the formula *vestigial creaturae in trinitate*, which emphasizes that while creatures are unable to reflect the Trinity, the Trinity has the power to reveal itself in creatures.[37] The central thesis of Metzger's work is that Barth is neither a sacramentalist nor a secularist, that he is neither a Catholic nor a liberal.[38] As he expresses the idea:

> In Barth's work the dedivinization of culture gives rise to the humanization of culture. This reality of dedivinization enables culture to be the human, creaturely reality as it is intended by God to be. And although Barth guards against the secularization of human culture by emphasizing the significance of the Word for the whole of creaturely reality, not simply the sacred sphere, he is still able to give space to culture to be truly secular in light of the Word. Dedivinization and desecularization spell humanization,

---

[33] George Hunsinger, "Karl Barth's Christology: Its Basic Chalcedonian Character," in *Disruptive Grace: Studies in the Theology of Karl Barth* (Grand Rapids, MI: Eerdmans, 2000), 136–37.

[34] Charles T. Waldrop, *Karl Barth's Christology: Its Basic Alexandrian Character* (New York: Mouton, 1984), 174.

[35] Paul Louis Metzger, *The Word of Christ and the World of Culture: Sacred and Secular through the Theology of Karl Barth* (Grand Rapids, MI: Eerdmans, 2003), 124n9.

[36] Ibid., 200.

[37] Thomas G. Dalzell, *The Dramatic Encounter of Divine and Human Freedom in the Theology of Hans Urs von Balthasar* (Berne: Peter Lang, 1997), 91n2. Dalzell also cites Philip Rosato, *The Spirit as Lord: The Pneumatology of Karl Barth* (Edinburgh: T & T Clark, 1981), 53–56, on this point.

[38] Metzger, *The Word of Christ and the World of Culture*, 116.

which in turn spells the celebration of authentic secularity. . . . His dual emphasis on the de-divinization and de-secularization of culture enables him to mediate between Christ and culture in such a way that broader culture is given the space to be truly secular in distinct though inseparable relation to the sacred, in and through the eternal Word who became flesh. [39]

The problem for a Catholic reading this paragraph is that it sounds precisely like it leaves the order of creation unaffected by the Incarnation, at least until the renewal of the cosmos at the end of time. For Catholics, the idea is not merely that we are saved by Christ, but that one of the fruits of redemption is the possibility of *theosis*, or deification. The idea of a de-divinized culture sounds to Catholic ears a little like a de-alcoholized cocktail—something potentially intoxicating that has had the active ingredient removed.

Although Martin D'Arcy didn't have the benefit of Metzger's research, he read Barth in a way that seems very close to the judgment of Metzger—although he drew a different value judgment about it:

Barth's meaning is that the Redemption has restored the world and that there are reflections of this new glory to be found in the works of man and of civilization. But the restoration belongs to another plane and will not be revealed until the last day. Till then it is hidden in God with Jesus Christ. The best that can be seen in the world is a reflection like the light reflected on a pool or mountain-side. Culture, he says, has its own worth and dignity, but it is "an exclusively earthly reflection of the Creation, which itself remains . . . lost and hidden from us." There is "no continuity between the analogies and the divine reality, no objective relation between what is signified and what really is; no transition, therefore, definable in terms of any progress, can be made between one and the other." Such an inflexible verdict rules out any hope of relating heaven and earth, grace and nature. History can never be more than a pastime. When the last trumpet sounds, all the works of man will fade out; they have no bearing on what then is to be revealed.[40]

---

[39] Ibid., 81.

[40] Martin D'Arcy, *The Sense of History: Secular and Sacred* (London: Faber and Faber, 1959), 172–73.

Jessica de Cou reads Barth in this way when she says that far too much has been made of the theological significance of Barth's Mozart essays. She argues that when Barth wrote about Mozart, he was being playful and ironic.[41] He thoroughly enjoyed Mozart but thought that what human beings received from Mozart was something related to the good of play. It was something absolutely human, not divine. Hence Barth's playful comment that the angels play Bach for God but, when they are home having fun by themselves, they play Mozart.

Evidence for something like D'Arcy's reading can be found in Barth's *Church Dogmatics* in his great indictment of Catholic theology on the grounds that it is obsessed with the word "and": "In all its shoots the theology which says 'and' derives from one root. If you say 'faith and works,' 'nature and grace,' 'reason and revelation,' at the appropriate place you logically and necessarily have to say 'Scripture and tradition.' The 'and' by which the authority of Holy Scripture is relativized in both Roman Catholicism and Neo-Protestantism is only the expression, one expression, of the fact that already the majesty of God has been relativized in His fellowship with man. And in this primary relativizing both are equally remote from the Reformation decision."[42]

Contrary to Barth, D'Arcy argued that, from the Catholic point of view, "nature and the supernatural action of God have been wedded together, and to divorce them is, however salutary the purpose, a desecration. The task of the Christian thinker is, therefore, to do justice to the marriage while accepting the very different roles, and even temperaments, of each member."[43] Specifically, D'Arcy endorses the idea of Abbot Butler that "the period between the two comings—the Incarnation and the Last Day—has a special mark like that on the doorpost of the Israelites on the night the Egyptians were smitten." The change effected by the Incarnation is a "prevenient grace, which prepares nature and dresses it for the time when all things shall be made new." Moreover, "the harvest to be reaped at the end of time is homogeneous with the historical seed, and in its growth that seed exercises its mysterious, biological alchemy on the inanimate matter wherein it has been placed."[44] According to Butler,

---

[41] Jessica de Cou, "Relocating Barth's Theology of Culture: Beyond the 'True Words' Approach of *Church Dogmatics* IV/3," *International Journal of Systematic Theology* 15, no. 2 (2012): 154–72.

[42] Karl Barth, *Church Dogmatics*, vol. 1/2, trans. G. T. Thompson and Harold Knight, ed. G. W. Bromiley and T. F. Torrance (Edinburgh: T. & T. Clark, 1956), 557 (nos. 13–24).

[43] D'Arcy, *The Sense of History*, 173.

[44] Ibid., 182–83.

whom D'Arcy admired, for a Christian, the purpose of life should not be to "pass through it, get it over, and arrive, without baggage but personally safe," but rather to arrive "at the final customs house . . . with all that he acquires along the road," and it is precisely what he has to declare that will "determine forever his enjoyment of the fatherland."[45] In D'Arcy's words, "toys in themselves are of no account, but to children they are so dear that they take them to bed with them; and when we go to sleep and awake to everlasting joy the toys of this life may well be part of our transfigured humanity. . . . What we do now prefigures what we shall do with complete happiness, even as the doll cherished by the child is the first love of the future mother."[46]

Butler acknowledged that cultural achievements can be the products of sinful desires or, as he expressed the idea, "embellishments not of the City of God but of Babylon." Nonetheless, he argued that the "potentialities which they thus not only actualize but deform are potentialities of ontological man and, as such, may participate in the 'resurrection' of grace. They and their products are therefore susceptible of supernaturalization and can be made to subserve the reign of God." To emphasize the point, he suggested that we "do not enjoy a few stray 'advances' upon our eventual inheritance. It is the whole of that future inheritance that is mysteriously anticipated in grace."[47]

With reference to the scriptural roots of these distinctions, D'Arcy suggests that Catholics and Barthians have different interpretations of St. Paul's *Letter to the Colossians* 1:20—that the Father is through Christ to reconcile all things in himself—and *Letter to the Romans* 8:20—that the creature was made subject to vanity and so on. D'Arcy also suggests that a certain ambiguity in the use of the word "world" and in the description of the City of Man obscured the question of whether nature and the good works of man were condemned to vanity or could be brought into relation with the supernatural order.

Not only are these differences significant at the level of what we make of our cultural achievements, but much more fundamentally, they are significant for what we make of the potentialities of a Christian humanism. Several authors argue that it is Barth's position that one cannot deduce anthropology from Christology. This, however, was precisely the central project of the pontificate of John Paul II: the development of a Christo-

---

[45] Butler, "The Value of History," 299.

[46] D'Arcy, *The Sense of History*, 211.

[47] Butler, "The Value of History," 298–99.

centric Trinitarian theological anthropology. In contrast, Philip J. Rosato, S.J., argued that, in Barth, anthropology is totally conceived of as the work of the Holy Spirit: "pneumatology replaces the concept of nature, reducing the human person to a passive bystander."[48] Rosato went so far as to assert that Barth was first and foremost a pneumatologist.[49] George Hunsinger implicitly concurs with Rosato:

> The work of the Holy Spirit, as Barth saw it, is miraculous in operation. The Holy Spirit is seen as the sole effective agent (*solus actor efficiens*) by which communion with God is made humanly possible. In their fallen condition (*status corruptionis*), human beings cannot recover a vital connection with God. Their minds are darkened, their wills are enslaved, and the desires of their hearts are debased. Through the proclamation of the gospel, however, the impossible is made possible, but only in the form of an ongoing miracle. This miracle is the operation of the Holy Spirit, not only to initiate conversion (*operatio initialis*), but also to continue it throughout the believer's life (*operatio perpetuo*). The only condition (necessary and sufficient) for new life in communion with God is the Spirit's miraculous operation in the human heart (*operatio mirabilis*). Faith in Christ, hope for the world, and consequent works of love have no other basis *in nobis* than this unceasing miracle of grace. Faith, hope and love, in other words, do not depend on regenerated capacities, infused virtues, acquired habits, or strengthened dispositions of the soul. Those who are awakened to lifelong conversion by the Spirit never cease to be sinners in themselves.[50]

Barth thereby objects to all theories that imply a "systematic co-ordination of nature and grace."[51] This rules out the Thomistic idea of a divine material cause cooperating with a human instrumental cause, and, as stated earlier in this essay, it rules out a sacramental ontology.

In the final analysis, the distance between the Barthian and the Catholic positions is quite wide because of the fundamental differences

---

[48] Rosato, *The Spirit as Lord*, 131.

[49] Ibid., 134.

[50] George Hunsinger, "Karl Barth's Doctrine of the Holy Spirit," in *The Cambridge Companion to Karl Barth*, ed. John Webster (Cambridge: Cambridge University Press, 2000), 183.

[51] See, for example, his famous "No!" essay.

in the areas of sacramental theology and ecclesiology, and even perhaps in Trinitarian theology, where there are different understandings of the role of the Holy Spirit in the economy of salvation. Barth seems to give the Holy Spirit rather a lot more work than is normally allotted by Catholic theologians. One can only amuse oneself with the thought of what Barth would make of the nuptial mystery theology of Ouellet and Cardinal Angelo Scola.

Nonetheless, it is the case that the Catholic theology of the Incarnation has to be held together with a theology of the Cross at one side and a theology of creation at the other, and in this sense, there is a strong affinity with Barth about the importance of the theology of the Cross. An example of what goes wrong when this end of the triptych is somehow occluded may be found in some of the loopy appropriations of John Paul II's Wednesday audience addresses on human love. These are now popularly marketed as his theology of the body. Some commentators so emphasize the effects of the Incarnation on the redemption of human sexuality that the problem of concupiscence is completely muted. There is reputedly a colony of hippies living somewhere in Montana who give up wearing clothes during the summer months on the grounds that they are implementing John Paul II's theology of the body principles. Barth and even Teilhard de Chardin would find that problematic.

Moving now from Barth to the Dutch Reformed tradition as expressed in the thought of Abraham Kuyper, we can begin with Kuyper's most famous line that "there is not a square inch in the whole domain of our human existence over which Christ, who is sovereign over all, does not cry 'Mine!'"[52] This statement resonates well with Catholics, who have never had a problem with the idea of Christ's sovereignty and even reserve a feast day to celebrate Christ's kingship. In 1903, Pope Pius X wrote a whole encyclical (*E Supremi*) on the subject of "restoring all things in Christ." The issue between Catholics and Kuyperians is one of how this sovereignty is exercised.

Kuyper believed that Catholics were right not to buy into the Lutheran "two kingdoms" concept, but he thought that the Catholic error was one of believing that Christ's sovereignty is exercised through the Church. Instead he favored the idea that the world can be carved up, so to speak, into different social spheres such as family life and professional life, and that in each of these spheres there are particular ways of respecting the sov-

---

[52] Abraham Kuyper, "Sphere Sovereignty," in *Abraham Kuyper: A Centennial Reader*, ed. James D. Bratt (Grand Rapids, MI: Eerdmans, 1998).

ereignty of Christ and particular precepts to be followed, with individual Christians doing the following: either honoring the precepts or violating them. The basic idea of spheres sovereignty is that each sphere has its own character and each is directly under the divine rule. According to Richard Mouw, Kuyper reads the "be fruitful and multiply" in Genesis 1:28 as a call to cultural activity or a "cultural mandate." Human beings are called to flourish in the kind of participation in created life that God intends for us. The effect of the Fall is that the modes of participation become either obedient participation or disobedient participation.[53]

Kuyper's concept of spheres sovereignty is not synonymous with the Catholic idea of "subsidiarity." Subsidiarity is a principle about decentralizing authority within spheres; it is not about the sovereignty of the spheres themselves. Nonetheless, subsidiarity is perfectly consistent with how Kuyper sees the work of individual Christians within the various spheres. Where Catholics are keen to emphasize that governments have no right to interfere with the authority of parents over the education of their children, Kuyper would agree wholeheartedly but add that the Catholic Church itself has from time to time in its history been guilty of similar incursions into spheres beyond its competence. Anyone who has ever worked for the Catholic Church would know that one of its problems is that people in ecclesial positions have a tendency to exercise authority in areas that are completely outside their competence. We need many more "dykes and dams," to use Mouw's metaphor, to make sure that people who have expertise in one field do not try to exercise it in another. There are numerous examples, but the most common are canon lawyers who try to handle public relations and diocesan business managers with expertise in property law and accounting who try to advise bishops about pastoral priorities. In the past, there were bishops who tried to use their theological authority to make judgments about scientific matters.

Kuyper died before the Second Vatican Council began, but it would seem that his idea of spheres sovereignty, or something very like it, was what the Council fathers were driving at in §36 of *Gaudium et Spes*: "If by the autonomy of earthly affairs we mean that created things and societies themselves enjoy their own laws and values which must gradually be deciphered, put to use, and regulated by men, then it is entirely right to demand that autonomy. Such is not merely required by modern men, but harmonizes also with the will of the Creator. For by the very circum-

---

[53] Richard J. Mouw, *Abraham Kuyper: A Short and Personal Introduction* (Grand Rapids, MI: Eerdmans, 2011), 7.

stances of their having been created, all things are endowed with their own stability, truth, goodness, proper laws and order."

This paragraph, or at least the bit about all things being endowed with their own "stability, truth, goodness, proper laws and order," is a paraphrase of statements made by both Aquinas and Augustine. It is perfectly capable of a non-self-secularizing interpretation. However, the use of the word "autonomy" has given rise to a variety of interpretations, most broadly the idea that God and the supernatural realm is one thing and the world and so-called secular realm is another, with the latter in a state of total independence from the former. In theological parlance, a relationship of total independence is said to be an "extrinsic" relationship, and there have been many populist interpretations of this paragraph that view the relationship as extrinsic.

Cardinal Angelo Scola has recently complained of precisely this problem. He has lamented that there is a latent ambiguity around the interpretation of the principle of the "autonomy of earthly affairs" mentioned in §36 of *Gaudium et Spes*. With reference to some of the interpretations of this paragraph, Scola suggested that it might be right to ask whether "the Catholic world, called to address the great contemporary anthropological and ethical challenges, has not been co-responsible, whether by naivety, delay or lack of attention, for the current [secularist] state of things."[54] According to Scola, §36 is an acknowledgement that there is a realm of life that is the responsibility of the laity (cf. the Council's Decree on the Apostolate of the Laity, *Apostolicam Actuositatem*, §7). This seems to be very close to Kuyper's position. The most significant distinction would be that the Church reserves to herself the competence to make judgments about matters of faith and morals that may have an impact in some particular sphere. Here the ruling against the use of contraception would be the most obvious example. The *communio* ecclesiology of the Second Vatican Council represents a move away from a strictly juridical account of the Church and toward a view that imagines the Church as a symphonic interplay of different spiritual missions, only one of which is the Petrine, the mission of ecclesial governance.

In the work of Balthasar—which represents the most extensive articulation of *communio* ecclesiology—the Petrine mission (the offices of pope, bishop, and priest) works in communion with other missions, in particular with the Johannine mission, which stands for the contemplative vocation,

---

[54] Angelo Scola, "El Peligro de una Falsa 'Autonomia,'" *Humanitas: Revista de Antropologica y Cultura Christianas* 66 (Fall 2012): 296–301, at 299.

the Pauline mission, which is one of prophetic utterance and evangelization, and the mission of St. James, which is one of defending the tradition and seeing that it is transmitted uncorrupted from one generation to
the next. Kuyper was writing before the Second Vatican Council, and so
the only Catholic Church he knew was one steeped in the ecclesiology of
the post-Tridentine theologians, and thus he cannot be criticized for not
appreciating the complexity and nuances of the *communio* ecclesiology.
There seems to be a very strong affinity between the *communio* understanding of how lay people mediate the grace of the Incarnation to the
world and Kuyper's ideas about the activity of Christians in various social
spheres. Thus, Mouw makes the point that Kuyper distinguishes between
the Church and the Kingdom: "The Kingdom . . . encompasses the believing community in all of its complex life of participation in a variety of
spheres. Whenever followers of Christ are attempting to glorify God in
one or another sphere of cultural interaction, they are engaged in Kingdom activity: a Christian art guild gathered for obedience in the sphere of
the arts; a Christian farmer's group gathered for obedience in the sphere of
agriculture; a Christian college or university gathered for obedience in the
world of teaching and research."[55]

Nonetheless, Kuyper was an avowed Calvinist. In his book *Calvinism* he wrote: "Lutheranism remained ecclesiastical and theological, it is
only Calvinism which both inside and outside the Church has left its mark
upon all forms of human life. No one speaks of Lutheranism as the creation of a distinctive way of living; even the name is scarcely mentioned,
whereas all who know history agree more and more in calling Calvinism
the creation of a distinctive world of human life." For Kuyper, a hallmark
of Calvinism is the immediate relationship between God and man. Like
Barth, there is no sacramental ontology. Kuyper specifically rejected the
idea of a church as a *Heilsanstalt* (institute of grace), and he thought that
one advance of Calvinism was that it is much more pluralistic about matters of ecclesial governance structures than the Catholic tradition. Whereas Catholics have a tendency to look at the thousands of different Protestant church structures and shake their heads with paternal tenderness,
Kuyper regarded this plurality as something to be affirmed and celebrated.

If Kuyper is right about Calvinism being a life form or a culture in itself, then this raises the question of how it differs from Catholicism and its
life form and culture. A paradox that first comes to mind when considering this question is that whereas the Protestant emphasis is on faith alone

---

[55] Mouw, *Abraham Kuyper*, 58.

and the Catholic tradition's emphasis is on faith and works, it is the Catholic tradition that ends up with a culture that is much more contemplative, much less work-oriented. Everyone agrees that there is a Protestant work ethic, but notwithstanding the efforts of George Weigel, the late Richard John Neuhaus, and the whole *First Things* journal, a Catholic work ethic has yet to socially arrive. Transposing this into Balthasar's *communio* terminology, we can say that, from the Catholic point of view, Calvinism represents a lopsided emphasis on the Pauline mission. There is prophetic utterance and evangelization, but there is only a very weak Petrine mission (no pope or bishops), no Johannine mission at all (that is, monasteries and convents for contemplatives), and only a very weak Jacobite mission (that is exercised through the leading scholars of the tradition). There is also no strong sense of sacramentality, no nuclear fission, and no relics of saints. Sociologists such as Swiss Werner Sombart have said that Calvinist cultures are bourgeois and that Catholic cultures are erotic. Sombart's point was that Calvinists are practical and efficient people while there is an out-of-control erotic element in Catholicism. This is what produces both the Catholic saints and the Catholic eccentrics. It is perhaps the difference between a view of an incarnational humanism as merely parabolic and one that is nuptial.

Jeremy Begbie argues that Kuyper tended to ground culture in the created order rather than in the order of redemption.[56] In this sense he is very much like Barth and, thus, a classical Calvinist. Other authors such as David VanDrunen argue that, for Kuyper, Christ exercises sovereignty over the world as redeemer rather than as Creator.[57] But even if this is so, it means that the emphasis is tipped to the theology of the Cross, not the theology of the Incarnation.

If we agree with Begbie, then we may say in summary that Kuyper puts weight on creation (which is perhaps where his openness to natural law ideas comes from, though that is another paper), that Barth puts weight on the eschaton (although the weight may have become lighter as he moved from the young Barth to the mature Barth), and that Ratzinger and other Catholic theologians put weight on the Incarnation, though of course the Incarnation remains suspended between the theology of creation and the

---

[56] Jeremy S. Begbie, "Creation, Christ, and Culture in Dutch Neo-Calvinism," in *Christ in Our Place: The Humanity of God in Christ for the Reconciliation of the World: Essays Presented to Professor James Torrance*, ed. Daniel P. Thimell and Trevor A. Hart (Allison Park, PA: Pickwick, 1991), 126.

[57] David VanDrunen, *Natural Law and the Two Kingdoms: A Study in the Development of Reformed Social Thought* (Grand Rapids, MI: Eerdmans, 2010), especially chapter 7.

theology of the Cross.[58] Fundamentally, there are different interpretations of what St. Paul meant about restoring all things in Christ so that He may be all in all, and different interpretations of what St. Peter meant about growing in the grace and knowledge of Christ.

Friedrich Nietzsche said that if Christians wanted him to believe in their redeemer, then they would have to start looking a lot more redeemed.[59] If, when people hear of Calvinism, they think of Ned Flanders from "The Simpsons," or if, when they hear of Catholicism, they think of Fr. Ted from the Irish comedy series, then there is no wonder that the world is full of Nietzscheans. The burden, from the Catholic side, is to show that a life spent participating in sacraments makes a significant difference to one's humanity.

---

[58] Peter McGregor argues that what is sometimes called Ratzinger's "preferential option for the Gospel of St. John" is due, at least in part, to the fact that St. John emphasizes the identity of *Logos* and *Agape* and thereby draws together the theology of the Incarnation with the theology of the Cross (*Heart to Heart: The Spiritual Christology of Joseph Ratzinger* [Allison Park, PA: Pickwick, 2016]).

[59] Friedrich Nietzsche, *Thus Spake Zarathrustra*, ed. by Adrian Del Caro and Robert Pippin (Cambridge: Cambridge University Press, 2006), 71.